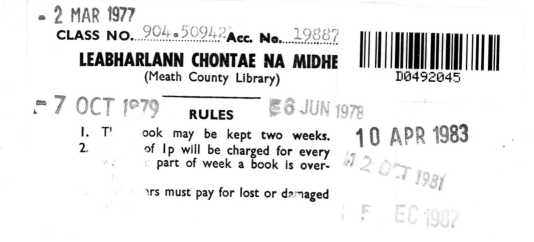

INGRID HOLFORD

BRITISH WEATHER
DISASTERS

DAVID & CHARLES
NEWTON ABBOT LONDON
NORTH POMFRET (VT) VANCOUVER

ISBN 0 7153 7276 9
Library of Congress Catalog Card Number 76-20117

Set in 11 on 12 pt Baskerville
and printed in Great Britain
by Redwood Burn Limited Trowbridge
for David & Charles (Publishers) Limited
Brunel House   Newton Abbot   Devon

Published in the United States of America
by David & Charles Inc.
North Pomfret   Vermont 05053   USA

Published in Canada
by Douglas David & Charles Limited
1875 Welch Street   North Vancouver   BC

CONTENTS

page

Author's Note   4

Acknowledgements   4

1 *Blow winds and crack your cheeks*   5
     Hatfield 1957/Ferrybridge 1965/Tay Bridge 1897/*Sea Gem* 1965
     Sheffield 1962

2 *The glass is falling hour by hour, the glass will fall for ever*   16
     But if you break the bloody glass you won't hold up the weather
     Glasgow 1927/Glasgow 1968

3 *The Lord hath his way in the whirlwind*   24
     Wisley 1965/Berkshire 1950/Widecombe-in-the-Moor 1638

4 *Now the great winds shoreward blow*   29
     Royal Charter storm 1859/The Great Storm 1703

5 *The rain descended and the floods came*   38
     Mossdale 1967/Norwood 1964/Surbiton 1973/Norwich 1912
     Molesey 1968

6 *What dreadful noise of water in mine ears*   52
     South-east Scotland 1948/Louth 1920/Devon and Somerset 1968
     Lynmouth 1952/Devon and Somerset 1960

7 *Snow on snow in the bleak mid winter*   69
     Snowdon 1972/Cairngorms 1971/Snowdon 1972
     Southern England 1891/*Ross Cleveland* 1968
     The winter of 1962-3/London 1814

8 *Like an army defeated, the snow hath retreated*   85
     Lewes avalanche 1836/Glazed frost 1940/River Till flood 1841
     Snow thaw floods 1947

9 *Have I not heard the sea puffed up with winds rage like an angry boar*   96
     London 1928/Scotland 1953/East Coast floods 1953

10 *The heaven is shut up and there is no rain*   117
     Fire of London 1666/London smog 1952/Motorway pile-up 1971

Bibliography   124

Index   126

AUTHOR'S NOTE

There are special problems about writing during the confusing period of conversion from traditional British units of measurement. Scientists already think in terms of metric units only. School-children learn the new system but live alongside the old with easy adaptability, but their parents still have a long struggle ahead before they can automatically visualise the new measurements. Obviously, I shall displease somebody whichever units I use and, since I feel that I may as well be hung for a sheep as for a lamb, I have decided to be inconsistent for what I believe are good reasons.

Temperatures are given in Centigrade, because this scale has been used long enough in weather forecasts to have become familiar.

Rainfall, depths of water and contour heights are in millimetres and metres because I think that by this time people will have accepted the conversion owing to the similarity between the metre and the old yard.

But as regards greater distances and wind speed, I have stuck firmly to miles and miles-per-hour, because these have practical reality to everyone through their motoring experience and I can detect no imminent move afoot to make the difficult change to kilometres.

Where it has seemed particularly incongruous to translate into units unknown to the original measurer, I have quoted direct from the era concerned.

ACKNOWLEDGEMENTS

This book could not have been written without reference to many detailed accounts of weather happenings by fellow meteorologists and authors, to whom I give thanks. I cannot add anything to their minute scrutinies but hope to have added a larger perspective to the general picture of weather disasters and their causes in Great Britain. I wish to thank the Director-General of the Meteorological Office for permission to use the library at Bracknell, and Mrs Cowlard for the magical way she produced from the bookshelves just what I wanted. Mr Caldwell of the Agricultural Development Advisory Service gave me great help in understanding the problems of salt in soil.

I must also thank the countless other people who have spent time and trouble talking to me about their calamitous experiences. Even if they recognise little of their particular accounts in the final text, I assure them that every word has contributed to the general picture of what the British people suffer from the weather.

INGRID HOLFORD

4

1

Blow winds and crack your cheeks

William Shakespeare

Although the weather is changeable, unpredictable in the long term and malignantly disposed to ruin events of importance, Great Britain is not a bad place to live in. Air temperature usually fluctuates within a narrow range which gives comfortable living conditions and rain is on average adequate for the production of varied crops. The islands are outside the latitudes cursed by the demon hurricanes, and there are no volcanoes breathing fire nor earthquakes of a magnitude to tumble cities.

Nevertheless, there are few catastrophes caused by the weather in other parts of the world which are not mirrored with equal impact by similar events in Britain. Death from cold is as final if it occurs at frost level or at many degrees below frost level, a collapsed roof is as devastating if achieved with wind of 80 mph or 180 mph, and the filthy invasion of homes by flood water and debris is equally sinister anywhere in the world.

Many tales of disaster, however, leave the uneasy feeling that the blame does not lie entirely with the weather but also with some coincident action or non-action of man. Watercourses become blocked, buildings are poorly maintained or badly built, and sometimes ignorance or plain thoughtless-ness are the real villains. For this reason, rather than a ghoulish interest in other people's misfortunes, it is useful to study each type of battle the weather has won so that unnecessary mistakes can be avoided in the future.

When preparing against any adversary advance warning of attack is helpful, but the task of meteorologists is unenviably difficult. So many variables in a three dimensional atmosphere are involved in weather forecasting that there are no precise mathematical answers. Nor are there ever likely to be, despite technical improvements for gathering and assimilating pertinent data. However, general weather patterns can be anticipated fairly accurately for several days ahead and though the finer details which set the scene for disaster often elude us, there is a certain similarity about potentially dangerous situations which make them worthy of recognition by everyone.

One weather factor is particularly useful in forecasting, and that is the pressure exerted by the air overhead. It varies daily and from one place to another, but if simultaneous values are plotted on to a map they produce a useful and simple forecasting tool. Lines called isobars are drawn joining places having equal pressure (after adjusting to an imaginary mean sea level) and these form fluid concentric patterns which blend one into another and indicate certain types of weather. More particularly, they indicate wind direction and strength, because air attempts the same manoeuvre as other liquids when confronted with uneven surface contours — it tries to move from a high level to a low level. In the case of air which is above the influence of surface friction, about 600 metres above ground level, the direction of movement is influenced by the rotation of the earth on its axis. There is a deflection of 90° to the right (in the northern hemisphere) from a straight-forward high-to-low direction. Wind blows in a direction parallel to the isobars, with low pressure on the left hand when you imagine wind on your back. The strength of the wind is inversely proportional to the distance between the isobars, so that the closer together the lines are the stronger is the wind. The actual speed can be obtained by merely placing a graduated scale at right angles to the isobars.

The snag here is that every weather chart merely shows a picture for one moment of time, but any weather situation is constantly changing. It is as hard for a forecaster to predict how it will develop as it is for a doctor to assess the development of an influenza epidemic. Even the simple rule of wind measurement seems a broken reed when you realise that what most people want to know is not the wind at 600 metres but at ground level. There, the drag of friction slows down wind by about 25 per cent, backs wind direction by anything up to 35° from the direction up above, stirs wind into turbulence and deflects it by obstacles, so that one is back again in the realm of hopeless complication. Despite all the reservations about isobaric charts, however, they are the very best weather alarms available and any newspaper

worth its salt publishes each day the most up-to-date version available at the time of going to press.

Long before man was able to formulate in words that wind is moving air which exerts a force, he learnt to cope with the problem on a trial and error basis. There were undoubtedly many collapsed homes before prehistoric man was able to leave the security of wind resistant caves and build safely, but gradually techniques evolved which suited the average wind conditions of different areas. On the north-western seaboard of Britain, for instance where an average thirty days a year produce gale winds of 40 mph or more, house walls have always been thicker than in central England where such winds probably occur on only five days of the year. The engineering problems of suspending roofs over walls are not so easily solved by the 'thicker-to-be-stronger' principle and must have been particularly difficult for early house builders. Relatively light-weight frameworks covered in thatch, slates or tiles are satisfactory protection against rain but have always been the weakest parts of buildings in high winds.

Hatfield   4 November 1957

After the war, when demand for new homes constructed cheaply and quickly stimulated many experiments with non-traditional materials, some 400 homes were built at Hatfield, Herts, with aluminium roofs of low pitch. It was a pleasant estate, imaginatively laid out, but the residents were not happy about their roofs, which heaved alarmingly in windy weather. Complaints to the authorities were shelved because there had been two years research before construction, and that seemed reasonable assurance.

In the early hours of Sunday 4 November 1957, many people on the estate

6

lay awake listening to the noise of a gale and the creaking in their roofs, torn between a desire to be proved right in theory and the more anxious desire to be proved wrong in practice. At 4am one man noticed his ceiling move up and down several inches and a few seconds later his roof peeled off. Part of the plasterboard ceiling collapsed into his room, just missing him, and the rest was deposited with the wooden framework into the garden. There was a blinding flash from a neighbouring house as the electrical wires were pulled away and another roof torn off, and then a further 24 roofs were stripped in like manner, leaving the terrified occupants exposed to the night sky. In all 26 other houses were damaged and three streets on the estate were strewn with wreckage.

No one was killed outdoors because at that hour everyone was at home. No one was killed in bed, because the roofs were sucked off rather than pushed inwards. This suction power is similar to that of wind flowing over the leading edge of an aircraft wing and it affects all leeward roof slopes and any windward roofs with a pitch of less than 30°, the worst affected being those less steep than 15°. The Hatfield roofs were of low pitch and needed meticulous fixing at ridges, corners and overhangs, all of which are particularly susceptible to suction and back eddies. Unfortunately they had not got this attention during building and the roofs were not even anchored firmly to the house walls, which made it easy for the wind to get its own way. All roofs on the estate were replaced or streng-

Low pitch aluminium roofs stripped from houses at Hatfield, Herts., during a gale on 4 November 1957. No one was killed outdoors because everyone was at home in bed; no one was killed indoors because roofs were sucked off rather than blown in. (*Building Research Station, Watford*)

thened by metal fixings to the walls and they have weathered many gales since, giving the occupants no more worries than anyone else has in wild wind.

An interesting feature of this disaster was that damage was confined to a compact area of the estate rather than affecting a random scattering of houses over the whole. It could have been that these roofs were worse fixed than the others but is more likely to have been the result of complicated turbulence in relation to other buildings, trees or contours. Everything nearby contributes to variations in wind pressure and the resulting arithmetic, different for every wind direction, is almost impossible to work out. Wind tunnel tests provide the best answer but it needed a dramatic disaster to emphasise that even these methods are not infallible.

Ferrybridge   1 November 1965

In 1965 eight cooling towers stood in staggered double file like giant sentries at the electricity generating station at Ferrybridge, Yorkshire. They appeared invincible, 115 metres high, 90 metres in base diameter and, above a slightly narrower throat, 55 metres across the top. Their sturdy exterior disguised the fact that they were merely empty draught tubes in which water fell from the top on to slats below in order to cool sufficiently for re-use.

On 1 November 1965, wind was blowing from W-WNW across the alignment of the towers and though the day was wild the wind speed was no more than must be expected once in every five years. The superintendent of the power station was working in his office when someone phoned to say that one of his cooling towers had fallen down. His immediate reaction was 'your're joking' but the message

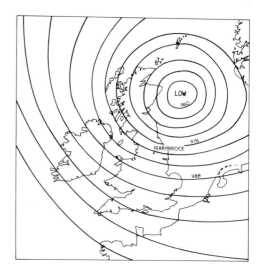

1200 GMT 1 November 1965. Average hourly surface wind at Ferrybridge, Yorkshire, was 44 mph with momentary gusts nearer 85 mph.

was quickly followed by a warning that another was about to collapse, which it did ten minutes later. The power station chemist, who also acted as photographer, grabbed his camera when he heard the warning and rushed out in the hope of getting a unique photograph. He photographed the second falling tower before discovering that in his excitement he had forgotten to remove the lens cap of his camera, and then joined anxious workers watching the remaining towers.

The wind got its own way forty minutes later. A third normally rigid tower appeared to become plastic and undulated like a sail caught aback in the wind. It ovalled and rippled just below the throat, then flexed 'as if a man were standing inside a bell tent and passing his hand horizontally round the inside of the fabric'. A hole appeared in the side of the tower, the top fell forward and the sides caved inwards to fill the water reservoir below. The photographer got his dramatic picture at the moment of collapse (opposite page). It was conspicuous that the three collapsed towers were in the leeward rank but later inspection showed that all the five towers which remained standing were also structurally damaged. It was a devastating thing to have happened in view of the fact that wind tunnel tests had been made before construction began, and a full enquiry was held.

I must now be more specific about gusts; these are momentary increases in wind which alternate with lulls around an average, but never constant, wind speed. Gusts occur because obstacles impede horizontal air movement and because there are also vertical movements of air which are caused by temperature change. The process is called convection, and it works like this. When an airstream moves over a warming surface, perhaps southwards over the sea into progressively warmer latitudes or over

The last of three cooling towers to collapse at Ferrybridge, Yorkshire, on 1 November 1965. Insufficient allowance had been made for turbulence between the close ranking towers and for the impact of even momentary gusts. *(Central Electricity Generating Board)*

ground heating in the sunshine, then the temperature of surface air rises as well. Being warmer it becomes lighter, rises upwards and is replaced by colder heavier air from above. The process continues till vertical up and down currents extend through often considerable heights of the atmosphere. Although upper air is free to move downwards from those imaginary tramlines of isobars on the weather maps, it still retains its direction and speed during descent, arriving at the surface as a gust veered about 30° from the average surface direction and considerably stronger. A gust may extend over only a few metres or over several hundred metres, depending on the vigour of the vertical air movement, and it will last only a few moments before being tamed by surface friction. But on a very gusty day, for instance when a north-westerly air stream moves southwards, the speed of a momentary gust may be twice as great as the average surface speed.

Unfortunately this is more serious than it sounds, because the *force* which wind exerts is directly proportional to the *square* of the wind speed. If a gust is twice the average speed then the force that gust exerts will be four times as great, and the higher the average speed the greater will be the danger of even momentary hammer blows by gusts. It is imperative not to smooth them into insignificance by considering statistical averages over long periods of time.

In the absence of any contrary ruling, the Ferrybridge cooling towers had been built to resist wind speeds averaged over one minute, which was then a normal British Standard allowance. The Ferrybridge station had no wind anemometer itself, but judging by records from a station 8 miles away, the maximum average *hourly* wind speed that morning was about 44 mph

9

near the ground and probably about 60 mph near the top of the towers. Averaged over a *minute*, the speeds were probably 54 mph and 75 mph respectively, but *momentary* gust strengths were thought to have been more like 85 mph and 103 mph respectively. The message was clear. Buildings such as these must be able to cope with the sort of wind speeds which could occur even once in fifty years over a duration period of at most 10 seconds. In fact, the safer averaging period of only 3 seconds is now often specified.

But there was more than this to the Ferrybridge disaster. The towers were built like giant chess pieces on a chequer board, only 100 metres apart, which was less than their own height. This was by no means a protective feature, for there is no provision in nature by which moving air can stop at any obstacle and politely give way to priority traffic. All the air merely crowds through whatever route is available and the increased amount has to move quicker in consequence. The narrower the constriction the more rapidly air must move, and at Ferrybridge the wind must have burst like cannon fire through the gaps in the first row on to the towers just beyond and caused their collapse. Back eddying and confused turbulence between the ranks contributed to the damage of the windward towers.

As soon as this theory was voiced the question arose as to why the wind tunnel tests prior to construction had not revealed the need for higher wind resistance. The answer was simply that the tests had been done on one model only which was therefore immune from the constriction effects of wind between several towers. It was a lesson learnt the hard way, and all wind tunnel tests on new structures now include as faithful a reproduction of the surrounding terrain and buildings as is possible.

The Ferrybridge towers were rebuilt or repaired to strengthened specifications and have been fully operational ever since. But in view of the complexity of wind behaviour, it is hardly surprising that engineers of past centuries, without the benefit of sophisticated laboratory equipment, also made some big mistakes.

Tay Bridge   28 December 1897
On the west coast of Scotland the river Tay descends from the Grampian mountains past Dundee towards the sea. The first Tay Bridge was started early in the 1870s as part of a project to link Edinburgh with Dundee, and was opened on 1 June 1878. The bridge was 2 miles long and the lattice of iron girders which rested on eighty-five brick bases just above high water level gave the bridge a light and airy look. Not everyone was happy about its strength, however, and one practising engineer felt so convinced that the bridge experienced undue vibrations that he reverted to using the ferry instead of the railway.

On Sunday, 28 December 1897, WSW gales were blowing across Scotland, reaching mean speeds of 60 mph at Aberdeen and Glasgow by 7pm and gusting between 80 mph and 100 mph. Dundee had no anemometer at that time but there is no reason to think its wind was materially different. The Tay Bridge had not experienced anything as violent as that before and the direction of the wind was broadside to its length.

The evening train set off across the bridge to Dundee and because it was Sunday there were only six coaches beside the brake van, and even those were not full. The signalman watched the retreating train and saw sparks which were probably caused by the wheels pressed hard against the leeward rails. The tail light disappeared round a bend and did not reappear again as usual. The Provost of Newport, who was anxiously watching the train because his son was a passenger, saw two great splashes of spray illuminated by a train light. The signalman tried to contact his opposite number but the line was dead, and when daylight came it was seen that part of the bridge had collapsed and the train had plunged with it into the water below, drowning all seventy-five people aboard.

An inquiry committee tried to piece together the reasons for the tragedy. The bridge had been passed as safe for a train speed of not more than 25 mph, but it became apparent that this had been accepted as an *average* speed and that the maximum train speed in the central section of the bridge was often much more. There was some evidence also that the standard of building workmanship had been less than perfect. One employee admitted that he had regularly packed and tightened loose tie bars which held the pillars together, but he did not pass on this information to his superiors who might have found it of uncomfortable significance.

The major fault in the structure, however, seems to have been that inadequate allowance was made for strong gusts. The designer admitted that he had given no particular thought to the matter beyond accepting in principle the arithmetic done by the Astronomer Royal concerning the proposed design for the Forth Bridge. Those calculations considered that though gusts of 40-50lb per sq ft might be possible in a storm they would bear on a strictly limited area of the bridge only and that the mean wind pressure over the long 1,600ft Forth spans would probably be in the region of

10lb per sq ft. The snag in applying these figures to the design of the Tay Bridge was that it ignored two factors. The Tay Bridge was a rigid construction with less sway to the wind than the suspension design of the Forth Bridge. And the Tay Bridge spans were only 227ft or 245ft long so that wind gusts would bear upon a far greater proportion of each span length than had been visualised for the Forth Bridge. This raised the potential *mean* wind loading over each span to much more than 10lb per sq ft in the case of the Tay Bridge. Though there was no verdict of culpable negligence, the enquiry decided that, even had the Tay Bridge been perfectly built and maintained, the margin of safety allowed for wind loading was greatly underestimated.

The error seemed obvious after the event but it must be remembered that knowledge of the complicated behaviour of wind was considerably less than it is now. To-day's designers must feel sympathy as they struggle with construction problems of new structures like oil rigs, which very name would be outside the comprehension of the engineers of the last century. The modern meteorological problem is not so much the behaviour of wind in its own environment but the behaviour it induces at secondhand upon the depths of the sea.

Sea Gem   27 December 1965
On 27 December 1965, the giant oil rig *Sea Gem* was at work in the North Sea about 40 miles east of the river Humber. A north-westerly wind was blowing at about 35 mph, developing waves 6 metres high on the surface and causing incalculable complications in water pressures on the underwater part of the rig. Suddenly one of the crew saw two of the drilling legs give way, the rig tilted and the deck soon

reached water level. It stuck for a while, some men managed to get away in boats, and then it collapsed and sank. Nineteen men were rescued from life rafts by a British ship, a helicopter winched 3 men from the water and 4 other men were at once known to be dead. That left 9 men still missing and the search continued for the rest of the day. Air temperature was only a degree above freezing and there was little chance for anyone to survive long in the very cold sea. There was a lingering hope that men could have survived in an air pocket within the sunken rig and frogmen tried hard to get close enought to the rig to investigate. But strong currents and turbulence, which stirred the bottom of the sea so that nothing could be clearly seen, prevented the divers getting nearer than 15 metres during the next couple of days. None of the trapped men survived, a poignant reminder that the more ambitious our building projects become the more we have to find out about the weather.

Sheffield   16 February 1962
The wind can play so many tricks that I doubt if we shall ever come to the end of the surprises. Sheffield, for instance, has suffered innumerable westerly gales over the centuries but had never had occasion to consider the close proximity of the Pennine mountains as a menace until 16 February 1962. In the early hours of that morning crazy winds were blowing from the Atlantic across Scotland, some places having mean hourly speeds over 65 mph, frequent gusts above 100 mph and Unst in the Shetlands reporting one gust of 177 mph. No one quite believes this figure but if it were even near that it would be fantastic.

Further south in the industrial belt of England there were also gales but not nearly so strong. Manchester,

Stockport and Rotherham were experiencing average winds of 45 mph—but Sheffield, sandwiched on the weather charts between the same spaced isobars, was suffering far worse than the other towns. Wind speed was about 35 mph at 4am but soon after 6am it increased to more like 75-80 mph with gusts up to 96 mph. Chimney pots, which are always lethal ammunition in gales, were crashing everywhere and killed three people; a crane 40 metres tall was uprooted and its huge jib crashed on to the new technical college; and many homes were blasted open to the night. A vicarage, with stone and brick lined walls nearly a third of a metre thick, was torn open at the gable so it was hardly surprising that the less robust estates of prefabricated homes took crippling punishment. Roofs lifted in every gust, many tore away, and a whole row of homes on one estate was razed to the ground. One family, sitting in their easy chairs because they were too frightened to go to bed, suddenly found only the front wall of their home standing. From 4am the fire brigade received calls for help at the rate of six a minute and when daylight came the city looked as if it had been struck by a wartime blitz. Some 100 homes were damaged beyond repair, a further 6000 were no longer weatherproof and about 100,000 others were damaged or suffered secondary troubles which appeared later. Everyone was exhausted after the terrifying night. It was still blowing hard and many parents who started to take children to school took them home again from sheer nervousness when they saw signs like the tangled knitting of scaffolding outside the college or the piano lying in the road without a house to cover it. Many of the children who did arrive at school were sent home for the simple reason that 100 of the 250 schools in

A builder's crane and scaffolding crumpled against the new Polytechnic building during the Sheffield gale of 16 February 1962. A chance combination of upper air factors and the windward barrier of the Pennines gave Sheffield much stronger winds than were experienced elsewhere. *(Courtesy of The Star, Sheffield)*

the area were damaged.

A reception centre was set up in the Town Hall which was manned for 24 hours a day to deal with enquiries; 120 homeless were accommodated temporarily at a secondary school and other people went to various church halls till they could contact friends or relatives for help. The city was declared a disaster area by the Government, and the Minister of Housing toured the stricken streets and promised that the country as a whole would help bear the cost of repair. The promise did not come till two days after the disaster and even then was not entirely unequivocal. Local authorities were urged to meet any costs immediately to carry out emergency work and the Government

would consider help if, after due attention to insurance, help was needed. It was then, and still is the national policy that local authorites should cope with such disasters and that central government should not get involved except to advise.

The best of co-operative attitudes prevailed locally. The building trade temporarily withdrew all union rules about not doing other people's jobs, the postmen called off their 'work to rule' campaign, and teams of builders arrived from other midland towns to help with an intensive repair programme. Each builder or group of builders was allocated an area and worked from house to house making them weatherproof, even if temporarily, along lines laid down by corporation officials. The operation was underwritten by the city treasury so that small builders could be paid weekly, and the supply of building materials was fortunately good. A relief fund was established and grew steadily to about £35,000 and from this applicants were given replacement goods. Cash awards were avoided as a precaution against non-genuine claims. The weather remained reasonably kind while temporary repairs were made, but it was months before all the scars were obliterated.

It was hard to explain why the usually reliable isobaric measurement of wind speed had been so wrong in Sheffield that day. Airstreams undulating over the top of the Pennines always give a constricting boost to wind speed on the heights, and turbulent eddying on the lee side as wind comes down again to valley level is a well known feature but was not enough to explain wind speed that day. The mountain range looms solidly to the west without any valleys tapering into the city to funnel the wind.

When physical contours alone failed

to deliver a sensible reason for the wind excesses, attention turned to the temperature contours of the air stream. There proved to have been an upper layer of air with temperature higher than the colder air beneath, a feature known as an inversion. Since cold air is heavier than warm air, this meant that the air pouring across the Pennines was deprived of any natural buoyancy which might have allowed the airstream to settle back quickly into its proper channels. On the contrary, the airstream bounced back from the upper lid of warm air like sound waves from a wall. The downward flip was transmitted to all the air below to give considerable compression near the ground. The air bounced back again from the ground and a pronounced vertical wave motion developed. At the bottom of the second trough, air which should have been spread out over a depth of $1\frac{1}{2}$ miles was squashed into a depth of less than one mile and consequently moving much faster than it should have done. By a chance in a million the length and amplitude of the wave motion, the height of the temperature inversion and the speed of the wind all combined to put Sheffield immediately below this trough. Surface wind was more like 80 mph than the 45 mph expected from the isobars, while only 9 miles downwind, underneath the next crest, the airstream had spread itself out so that surface wind was only about 18 mph.

This explanation sounds simple after the event and was amply supported by observations of the sort of lenticular wave clouds which form in these

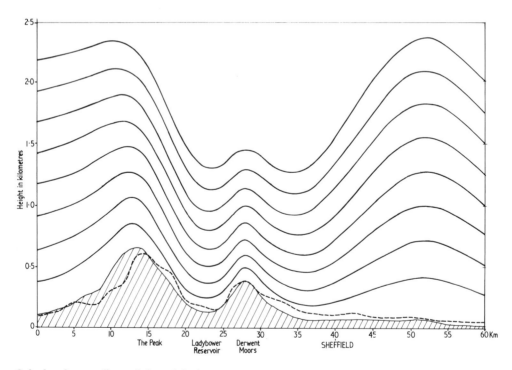

Calculated streamlines of air undulating across the Pennines in the vicinity of Sheffield in the early morning of 16 February 1962. The actual terrain contour is indicated by the dotted line, the effective terrain as used in the calculation is shown by the shaded area. *(Courtesy of the Director General, Meteorological Office, Crown copyright)*

14

upper air conditions, but to *forecast* such an occurrence again is far from simple. It would need an exact repeat of wind and temperature structure in three dimensions and to predict this is a problem to daunt the most experienced forecaster or the most sophisticated computer. The disastrous combination of circumstances has only happened once and may never happen again, and it seems debatable if the odds are significant enough to be considered when laying down local building specifications. It is *possible* to make every home resistant to wind speeds such as occurred in Sheffield in 1962 but it is hardly economic to do so if the freak conditions are unlikely to happen again. Certainly the Sheffield disaster could hardly have been considered a fair test of prefabricated homes in normal weather conditions.

2

The glass is falling hour by hour, the glass will fall for ever
But if you break the bloody glass you won't hold up the weather

Louis MacNeice

Gales nearly always occur in the anti-clockwise air circulations round centres of low pressure, called depressions. Since the most vigorous of these tend to prefer tracks north of the British Isles, so bringing the country into the southern half of the circulation, it was more than coincidence that all the disasters recounted so far occurred with wind directions between SW and NW. These are gale prone directions.

Nor was it difficult, with the peculiar exception of the Sheffield disaster, to portray the outdoor windy conditions by a weather map crowded with isobars orientated according to the relative position of the passing centres of low pressure. Actual measurements of pressure would have been pouring in by teleprinter to the Met Office with a time lag of up to an hour only for British stations. All that was necessary was to plot these values and draw the isobars, and the map mirrored the conditions outside.

It is a much greater problem to anticipate many hours ahead how the pattern of isobars will change, perhaps from wide spacing to close spacing. Depressions are subject to unpredictable whims and they not only travel but can change character with extraordinary speed. When they are in lazy mood they have a not very low depth,

and slack winds give the weather charts an indecisive appearance. Then suddenly they can deepen to become systems of great violence. Pressure falls more rapidly at the centre than on the periphery, the pressure gradient gets steeper, the isobars nudge closer together to indicate rising wind speed. If this happens close to Britain's shores it is often hard to spot the development before bad weather actually arrives, but if the depression develops on the other side of the Atlantic there is a better chance of tracking it and making an estimated time of arrival based upon speed and direction of travel. Forecasters always watch slack depressions very carefully for tell-tale falls in pressure which might indicate their revival.

Glasgow   28 January 1927
Glasgow is situated in a region which expects gusts of wind up to 100 mph once in every fifty years, and is close to the Western Isles whose winds are more likely to reach 120 mph with the same frequency. Local building methods have taken account of that fact, yet twice in this century the city has suffered unexpectedly widespread gale damage.

On Friday morning, 28 January 1927, the isobars were tightly packed

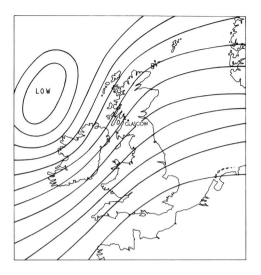

0600 GMT 28 January 1927. The peak of the storm on the Clyde estuary was during the afternoon when wind frequently gusted between 70 and 80 mph. Glasgow may well have had higher unrecorded gusts.

across the weather map and indicating average wind speeds of 55-60 mph over the north of England and Scotland. Wind direction was from SW-W over all the British Isles and during the day damage was reported from everywhere.

On the Clyde estuary the storm reached its peak during the afternoon, when wind was frequently gusting to 70-80 mph and soon after 4pm Paisley recorded a gust of 102 mph, the highest since records started there in 1883. Glasgow was a dangerous place to be in. The bonnet of a bus was torn off and hurled into a shop window, a tramcar toppled over and just missed crushing a girl who had been blown to the ground, and trees crashed on to overhead wires and disrupted electricity supplies. In the city centre the wind demolished a large business property piece by piece. First, part of the roof collapsed and men tore at the rubble in choking dust to uncover a boy buried beneath. Then the gable collapsed, a floor opened up and

everything crashed to the basement below, mercifully just after the building had been evacuated of people. Finally, the front of the building swayed, held till rescuers got quickly to safety, and then fell inwards to seal the fate of one man still buried under earlier rubble.

In the poorer tenement areas the chief instruments of destruction were the chimney stacks, which were tall because of the steep pitch of the roofs. They toppled into the streets and killed people outdoors, or they crashed through the roofs and made indoors just as dangerous. One stack fell clean through three floors carrying on an avalanche of bricks a sixty-year-old woman who was miraculously unhurt because she was cushioned by soft items of upholstery. Another chimney demolished the stairway of a building so that occupants could neither leave nor be certain the rest of the house was not about to collapse. They were rescued eventually by firemen whose ladders swung alarmingly in the wind and made the rescue of an old lady of eighty-seven particularly perilous. She was lowered in a sling which spun in semicircles as spectators below held their breath for her safety.

Eleven people were killed in Glasgow that day and over 100 were injured, and a further 15 deaths occurred in other parts of Scotland.

Forty-one years later the newspaper reports from Glasgow were hardly distinguishable from those of 1927.

Glasgow   15 January 1968
In the early hours of Sunday morning, 15 January 1968, storm winds were blowing from WSW across Scotland and northern England. Prestwick on the Scottish west coast recorded a gust of 96 mph, Tiree in the Western Isles and nearer the centre of the storm, had a gust of 117 mph; and at Great

Dun Fell in Westmorland, over 2,000ft high there was an authenticated gust of 134 mph. At Glasgow airport, several miles to the west of the city, average wind speed between 2am and 3am was 61 mph and one gust reached 102 mph—the roof of a hanger was blown off and lounge windows blown in.

Along the Clyde conditions were impossible. A lifeboat shed was turned upside down with the boat inside also inverted but undamaged; two 400ft pylons straddling the river collapsed and their heavy wires blocked access to shipping for many hours; and at Greenock a 723-ton dredger broke from her pier moorings taking with her a hopper barge tied alongside. The two vessels ground together, uncontrollably adrift, till the dredger sprang a leak and started to fill, eventually toppling over and snapping the ropes to the hopper. She floated for a while with part of her hull visible but sank before any attempt could be made to rescue the three men trapped inside.

In Glasgow the wind went beserk. It buckled a high crane which fell against a block of flats under construction; it blew away the frontage of four flats; and it totally wrecked three churches. And the chimney pots were again taking their toll. One car was squashed flat by a direct hit, another was just visible surfacing like a submarine from a sea of bricks. A chimney crashed a four-month-old baby in her pram through a top floor and it took neighbours and police an hour to dig her out unhurt, and a married couple were saved from their falling roof only because of a cross beam which jammed across their bed. Another stack went clean through two floors of a tenement house killing two mothers and two children and plunging furniture and belongings all to the ground floor. Forlorn curtains and a crazily balanced chair on the top floor were

Crashing chimney stacks became lethal weapons during high winds. This home was wrecked in Glasgow on 15 January 1968 and two mothers and two children were killed. *(Glasgow Herald and Evening Times)*

the only reminders that the house had just been lived in.

From 1am onwards 'Emergency 999' calls were puring in at such a rate that one GPO official accused people of abusing the system for trifling matters. It was an understandable opinion from someone who knew what was going on elsewhere, but there was no way that other people could know that their normally reasonable calls for help were in fact relatively minor on that night. The police worked continuously all night with firemen, servicemen and householders, making sensible and authoritative decisions on their own initiative and achieving miracles. They evacuated several families hurriedly just before a gable end of a tenement building crashed down and demolished a smaller house below; they cleared over 100 people from flats which were deemed to be in danger from a precariously leaning crane nearby; and the night staff of a geriatric hospital made up 250 beds in $1\frac{1}{2}$ hours to accommodate the homeless. A rest centre was opened in the town hall and everyone had safe shelter before the night was out. Nine people were killed that night in Glasgow alone.

Next day the unnerving vista of damage, particularly in the districts of Patrick and Maryhill, revealed obvious jobs to be done right away. The Corporation organised that dangerous buildings were either secured or pulled down, loose bricks were removed from roofs before they could again become flying missiles, trees and rubble were removed from roads and railways in order to get traffic moving again, and electricity was restored wherever it had been cut off. Forty-one families were rehoused by the evening and the rest were found temporary accommodation so that no one had to spend the night in the rest centre. It was a magnificent achievement which could hardly have been bettered by any preconceived plan, for the simple reason that no one can know beforehand just where disaster will strike.

Rehabilitation and aftercare were another matter. Glasgow Corporation was faced with a problem which grew every hour as assessment of damage poured in. The estimates of homeless people swelled from 600 on Monday morning to 1700 by Tuesday. First reports of 52 collapsed buildings, 997 chimneys broken and 423 roofs damaged later consolidated into the overwhelming fact that over 100,000 homes were damaged, many were not even weatherproof and by Tuesday it was raining. Furniture and fittings which had survived the gale were being ruined by water.

An alert had been given to the army whose mobility, wireless communication system, technical skills and simple chain of command make it ideally suited to help in times of disaster. By 8am on Tuesday a contingent of infantry from Edinburgh was waiting on the outskirts of Glasgow and sappers in Yorkshire were preparing to move north, everyone eager for the opportunity to infuse realistic purpose into their peacetime existence. Conferences were held in the Lord Provost's Office during which civilian caution over sensitive democratic procedures compromised gradually with more aggressive military pressure for dictatorial decisions. The army was going to use 7000 tarpaulins and was willing to shelve the problem of who paid—such items were accountable to the Ministry of Defence, though men and equipment could be lent freely for emergencies. There were suggestions at first from unions that repairing roofs was a job for slaters and carpenters only, but objections melted away as the immensity of the task became apparent and under the argument that many sappers were also qualified tradesmen. The political question about whether private property should be treated the same as council property was dropped when it was realised that the only way to work was to start at one end of a row of roofs and work steadily along to the other end, without stopping to enquire into the credentials of the people living below.

By Tuesday afternoon the infantry were collecting furniture and valuables from unsafe or roofless houses and churches and storing them in army drill halls. At dawn on Wednesday the sappers were off the ground, each man roped to another on either side of the roof ridges, moving steadily along to cover the gaping holes with the green tarpaulins and wooden battens which gave the city such a bizarre touch of colour for weeks to come. Later, as experience was gained, even the military band went aloft to do this job so that repairs needing more skilled attention could be dealt with by the engineers. The army stayed in Glasgow for two weeks making temporary repairs to over 1000 roofs, by which time the civilian organisations were able to cope on their own. A storm damage office was opened to co-ordinate rebuilding during the following months and flying squads went out on demand to attend to emergency repairs. When finally the permanent repairs were finished, some four years later, the storm damage office was retained as an advice centre for people displaced by redevelopment.

It was a pity that the excellent work of the Glasgow Corporation was marred by uncertainty about money. The extent of damage was far too great to be covered by local finance alone, and a junior official from Whitehall who flew to Glasgow on the Monday had no power to authorise money there and then. The Secretary of State a few days later offered Scottish local authorities and voluntary organisations 'all practical help that Government resources can provide in caring for the homeless and clearing debris'. But not until ten days after the disaster did he announce an immediate advance of £500,000 from the Contingency Fund as an instalment of Exchequer help. Long before that a feeling of neglect had grown in Glasgow which even led to an accusation in Parliament that Whitehall was more concerned with dead English seagulls than live Glaswegians. It was a travesty

of the truth only because of the nationalistic overtones. The same complaints had been voiced many times before in other weather disasters from John o'Groats to Lands End, and the fault lay in the system rather than in any local prejudice. Any town which suffers to the extent that Glasgow did needs and deserves the same sort of attention that a patient suffering from shock gets in a hospital, and in the case of a whole community an immediate dose of financial help is as good a tonic as any.

It was unfortunate also that on 15 January 1968 nature really went to town with disasters. There was severe flooding all over southern England where rivers, swollen by thawing snow, were piled over their banks by the westerly gales. The oil rig *Sea Quest* was adrift in the North Sea after losing her anchors in the heavy seas and, on top of everything, Sicily had its worst earthquake since 1908 — 430 people were known to be dead, thousands of buildings were in ruins and the Royal Navy dispatched several vessels to the island's aid. All these disasters shared the attention of the public and some Glaswegians found it hard to accept that foreign news should supersede mention of their own troubles in the BBC's evening bulletin. It was a touchy but natural reaction which could have been avoided had the city only had the undivided attention of one person with authority in Whitehall.

Since that time, the Local Government Act of 1972 has made special provision for times of emergency or disaster, or occasions when they may reasonably be expected. Local authorities may spend what they consider necessary up to an amount of 2p in the £ of their rating figure for the area, providing they do not usurp the functions of any other public body. They must at once notify the Secretary of State about what they are doing but since he may countermand their actions it still remains essential that quick confirmation be given by the central Government with assurances of grant aid where appropriate.

The 1968 Glasgow storm was universally termed a hurricane, a reasonable colloquialism for what was actually a very deep depression with average winds within the 'storm' category of 55-63 mph but gusting continually well above the minimum 'hurricane' level of 74 mph. In fact, the true hurricane is a feature of the tropical oceans, smaller in cross section than depressions of higher latitudes but much fiercer. Wind blows in almost circular anti-clockwise motion at all heights and surface speeds may be anything up to 200 mph. Centrifugal force holds back spiralling walls of rain bearing cloud from the central 'eye' of the hurricane, where subsiding upper air warms by compression and causes a phenomenal drop in atmospheric pressure at ground level. Little cloud exists in this warmer dry core so that people battered below by the first half of the hurricane are rewarded in the 'eye'

with a glimpse of sunshine or stars. Even more important, they get a temporary lull in wind, to about 10-15 mph which affords them an opportunity to make emergency repairs or to seek out better shelter. One thing is certain: the respite passes, the atmosphere pressure starts to climb as spectacularly as it previously fell and the hurricane winds renew themselves from the opposite direction.

Hurricanes in the southern Atlantic usually travel westward at first and then recurve towards the north-east. Their staple diet is warm moist air over the sea and once they reach land their end is in sight. Drag of friction causes surface winds to converge towards the centre, upcurrents and clouds invade the 'eye', and the hurricanes become familiar depressions of higher latitudes. The most vigorous depressions are not necessarily those with a past history as hurricanes but they often exhibit enough hurricane symptoms to suggest that the dividing line between the two types of low pressure systems is somewhat blurred.

The Glasgow depression started life on 12 January as a small wave on a trailing front across the Atlantic, at

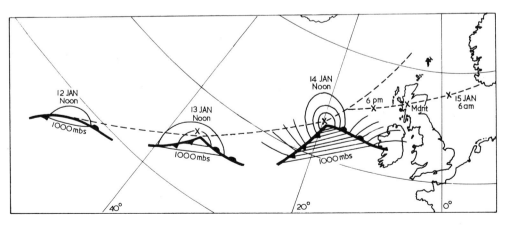

Development of a deep depression which caused widespread damage in Glasgow on 15 January 1968. Tornadoes probably existed in the forward part of the storm. Note the change of track to a more easterly direction than had been anticipated.

about 50°W. Forecasters viewed it warily, wondering if it would fizzle out or take over from the parent depression south of Greenland. It was destined for power. By midday on 13 January it had become a recognisable circulation with a centre at 40°W and a depth of 1000 mbs and was moving steadily north-east and deepening all the time. By midday on 14 January it had a depth of 972 mbs and was centred about 20°W on a latitude level with northern Ireland. The depression appeared to be decisively set upon its north easterly course and forecasters estimated the centre would pass well clear of Scotland, probably over the Faroes. Then, with the same capriciousness, it changed its mind. It altered course towards the east and by the time the 6pm weather charts were completed it was obvious that the earlier forecast was inaccurate. By midnight the depression was over Ross and Cromarty at a depth of 957 mbs; by 6 am on the 15th it was 956 mbs and half way across the North Sea towards southern Norway.

It was bad enough for Glasgow to be so close to the centre of such a deep depression, but it probably made matters worse that the city was situated in the right hand forward quarter of the system. This is where both hurricanes and deep depressions tend to spawn tornadoes, miniature versions of themselves with whirling spirals of air perhaps only a few metres or tens of metres in diameter. They have very low pressure at the centres and can suck off roofs or cause buildings to explode because of the inequality of pressure inside and out. Wind speeds near the centre have never been measured because no conventional instrument can stand the buffeting, but speeds are 'guesstimated' at 200-250 mph and have been known to move a 90-ton engine 55 metres along a railway line.

Vertical upcurrents round the centre are strong enough to pick up haystacks and set them down, often relatively gently, on the outer periphery of the circulations. The twisting motion of the wind tears out shallow-rooted trees or twists off the tops of those deeply enough rooted to remain anchored to the ground.

Though tornadoes have devastating impact upon everything over which they pass, their influence is limited to their immediate small cross section. They may crumple one row of houses yet leave an adjacent row untouched. From the roof tops of Glasgow the soldiers mending the gaping holes commented on the swathe-like appearance of the destruction cut through the town. The presence of tornadoes during the height of the storm would also account for the particularly vicious damage in the districts of Patrick and Maryhill, while inhabitants about 10-15 miles east of the city were hardly affected.

Further confirmation that tornadoes were present that night came from someone who lived in a solid sandstone tenement in the highest part of the city where high winds are no novelty. 'The storm lasted for two hours at a high intensity. The noise was tremendous but there were four quite distinct bursts of extraordinary violence. Each time we heard them coming from the west like an express train, the noise increasing all the time till they struck the building with an impact which could be felt. The structure seemed to move bodily.' It was a classic description of tornado noise.

The depression which caused the damage in Glasgow in 1927 was very similar to that of 1968, and on both occasions a trail of destruction was laid throughout the whole of Scotland and northern England and Ireland. In neither case did any other town suffer anything comparable to the punishment inflicted upon Glasgow. Admittedly the city had more than its fair share of old property and by 1968 the advent of smokeless fuel had caused chimneys to be less often swept, inspected and repaired. But damage in Glasgow was by no means confined to old property and other towns had their share of that too, so it is pertinent to consider if there is some peculiarity about Glasgow's situation which makes it particularly susceptible to wind disasters.

The city sits in a dish of low ground surrounded by mountains. The Clyde tapers in between high ground from the west; there is a sizeable valley running from the Firth of Clyde via Beith to open out on to Johnstone, Paisley and Clydebank, and another minor valley leads from the south-west to Barrhead and central Glasgow. These routes all offer constricting funnels for any winds from the south-west quarter of the compass and the turmoil of air bursting into the Glasgow basin during the 1927 and 1968 storms must have been fantastic. Moreover, the fact that the wind must have been channelled into the area from slightly different directions could have given just the shearing effect on the vertical winds near the centre of the depressions to set off tornadoes. It could well be that the city's complicated topographical surroundings make it prone to excessive wind when violent depressions pass near by.

When a disaster occurs like the 1968 Glasgow storm, it is a relief to blame someone and pretend that the trouble could somehow have been avoided. The Meteorological Office was blamed for not having warned the city that the depression would pass so close and the forecasters took their punishment as whipping boys with their usual stoicism. But if their acceptance of such a role is not to wear thin, the limitations not only of forecasting but of evading the weather must be appreciated by the public. Any forecast can only be the best possible estimate on the data available. It must be wrong sometimes but is hardly ever wrong through negligence. The alteration of course in the depression track in 1968 was quite unpredictable; when it was known, it was broadcast in the shipping bulletins for the benefit of vessels which could take avoiding action. Tornadoes develop suddenly and in unpredictable places, so that to wake a city in the middle of the night to warn that tornadoes *might* happen could be merely 'crying wolf'. One cannot move a home out of the way; one might get out of a house which remains safe and end up right in the narrow path of a destructive tornado, it serves no purpose to worry about something which may never happen. If hurricanes and tornadoes were a regular feature of British life then it would be worth while constructing windproof shelters for everyone. But when they are as rare as they are in Britain then the most sensible measures are to pay particular attention to maintenance and provide the very best of aftercare for the victims if the worst should happen.

3

The Lord hath his way in the whirlwind

Nahum 1.3

Although a steep pressure gradient *always* indicates strong wind, slack pressure gradient does not always guarantee calm air. Tornadoes can also occur when there is hardly an isobar decorating the weather map of the whole country. The reason, like that on the occasion of the Sheffield disaster, lies in the upper atmosphere. When there is a slack low pressure system over the country in spring or summer very strong vertical upcurrents may be triggered off by the sun. The shearing effect on these of comparatively light horizontal pressure winds seems to be enough to set some of them spinning as tornadoes.

Since these strong vertical currents also breed deep shower clouds which mask the sun by the afternoon and produce thunder, lightning, hail and heavy rain, the occasions when tornadoes occur as well can be awe inspiring. Meteorologists still have a great deal to learn about the whys and wherefores of tornado formation, so we must not laugh too scornfully at the old idea that they were manifestations of the wrath of God. The episode at the Wisley Horticultural Society Gardens on 21 July 1965 would, in a past era, probably have been considered punishment for the original misdemeanour in the Garden of Eden!

Wisley   21 July 1965

There had already been thunderstorms that afternoon, but when one had ceased soon after 3pm RHS students went out into the fields and orchards to continue their work. They noticed something approaching which they thought was a flock of birds, but as it got closer they realised it was a hollow tube of cloud extending down towards the ground from the main cloud base. This is a very usual way for a tornado to advertise itself and in daylight offers a useful visual warning to get out of the way. As the cloud got closer the 'birds' were seen to be bits of stick and debris caught up in the spiralling wind and everyone fled out of its path to safety. The tornado cut a trail of destruction between 10 and 30 metres wide through the countryside. Fruit trees in the orchards were tilted or torn out of the ground; one remained upright but had its roots exposed all around its trunk, and fruit was scattered everywhere. Along the main road substantial trees of about 2-3 metres in girth were split or had their tops twisted off. There had been no particularly strong gusts of wind preceding the formation of the funnel cloud though it was noticed that the ragged clouds below the main base were drifting in a variety of directions.

24

A tornado has a small enough cross section to impose its whole circulating wind pattern upon one tree which happens to be in the path. At Wisley on 21 July 1965 this peach tree had its top twisted off and carried 12 metres away, while the fruit trees in the background were quite unharmed. *(R. P. Scase)*

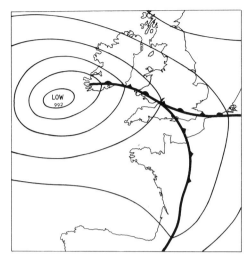

1500 GMT 21 May 1950. Tornado travelled nearly 100 miles, Berkshire to Norfolk, between 1600 and 2000 GMT.

The whole life span of the tornado only lasted about ten minutes and it only travelled a distance of about 2 miles. The path plotted according to observed destruction showed a zigzag course with one sharp right-angled bend — quite unpredictable.

Berkshire   21 May 1950

In comparison with the Wisley tornado, the one which originated in Berkshire on 21 May 1950 was a record for Great Britain. There was slack low pressure over south-east England, there were two main air masses feeding into the area, one from the north-east off the North Sea and the other warmer air stream from north Africa

via France. Deep clouds had built up during the morning and thunderstorms were occurring sporadically during the early afternoon. It was dark and gloomy in the Leighton Buzzard churches as the Sunday afternoon services drew to a close.

About 4pm a tornado was sighted in the valley running north from Great Missenden to Wendover. As it emerged from the valley it was probably given a further spin by encountering wind of a slightly different direction and it increased in ferocity and headed towards the north-east. People at the RAF station at Halton watched the funnel cloud approach, sucking things up into its base and fanning out at about 100 metres into the main cloud like some shadow palm tree. It lifted the roof off the camp power station, trampled an anticlockwise dance in the stinging nettles and screamed on to cut a narrow but severe trail of destruction through Aston Clinton. From thence it moved on to Puttenham where a well built pig byre exploded under the sudden reduction

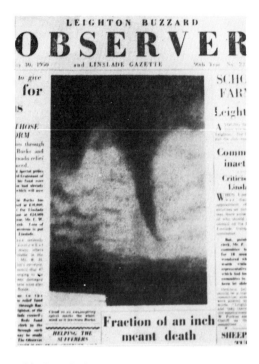

LEIGHTON BUZZARD

OBSERVER

and LINSLADE GAZETTE

Fraction of an inch meant death

This funnel cloud advertised the presence of a tornado which crossed Berkshire and travelled eastwards to north Norfolk on 21 May 1950. *(Beds and Bucks Observer)*

of outside pressure and the floor of a collapsed nissen hut was lifted 15 metres into the branches of a tree.

On the outskirts of Leighton Buzzard, at Linslade, the tornado almost entirely unroofed two roads of houses and contemptuously tossed aside parked cars. Slates and sheets of corrugated iron were flying about in the air in company with a cat, all four legs spreadeagled in an automatic balancing reaction to the new art of flying. Television aerials were twisted like corkscrews and some poultry were plucked clean of feathers as if ready for the oven.

The tornado blew open doors at Lidlington and sucked things out into the garden. It arrived south of Bedford soon after 5pm, visited the Fen district between 6pm and 7pm and finally dispersed at Blakeney on the north coast of Norfolk about 8pm. That was a total of nearly 100 miles in four hours, whereas the record known track

The Berkshire tornado of 21 May 1950 progressed across country in a series of kangaroo hops. Wherever it lowered to the ground it caused a trail of damage, particularly at

Linslade, near Leighton Buzzard, where two rows of houses were almost entirely unroofed. *(H. C. Griffin)*

26

for any tornado in Europe is 300 miles. The spiralling winds did not reach the ground for the whole of that distance but progressed with their funnel cloud across the countryside in a series of kangaroo hops leaving an erratic trail of chicken coops, sheds and scattered trees wherever it reached ground level. Its timetable was pieced together by meticulous detective work by H. H. Lamb of the Met Office. He noticed that the main bursts of energy were nearly always on the far side of ridges of hills where the tornado might have encountered slightly different horizontal wind directions, and that the tornado tended to break up on the approach slopes of hills, over tight coppices and avenues of trees. There were probably two other tornadoes at the same time following parallel tracks towards the north-east but not so long lived.

By deduction from the facts accumulated, it was estimated that wind speed near the centre could have been about 230 mph, and for this to have occurred the fall in pressure about 20 metres from the centre could have been about 30 mbs and at the actual centre perhaps several hundred millibars. To put this in perspective, the total range of pressure which covers all normal weather conditions is only about 100 mbs between very deep depression and very high anticyclones. If an ordinary barograph had been able to record under the tornado, the pen on the recording drum would have gone right off the bottom end of the scale.

On this occasion there was little loss of life directly attributable to the tornado apart from a number of poultry. Cattle seem to have been frightened out of the path of the tornado by the approaching noise 'like a train'. However, four people died because of lightning strikes and also quite a few cattle, and the torrential rain and hail which occurred during the storms preceding or following the tornado made it a thoroughly expensive demonstration of power.

Widecombe-in-the-Moor
21 October 1638

Whatever the final theory of tornado formation proves to be, electrical charges will be part of the explanation, either as cause or effect. Since church steeples provide lightning with its easiest route to earth it is not surprising that some of the more dramatic reports come from ecclesiastical sources.

On 21 October 1638 a thunderstorm was raging over Dartmoor and the Rev George Hyde was competing against it for the attention of his congregation in the parish church at Widecombe-in-the-Moor. It was very dark inside and many people were already apprehensive on that account when there was a vivid flash, a specially loud crack of thunder and part of the church roof fell in, littering the interior with rubble and filling the air with dust. There was a strong sulphurous smell, many people had their faces blackened and were badly burnt and a few had their clothes stripped off. The money in the purse of one man was partly melted. Four people were killed and about sixty others injured.

There was little doubt in the minds of local people about the reason for the disaster. The landlady of a nearby inn testified that the Devil had passed by and called for a drink, and she knew it was the Devil because the drink sizzled as it passed down his throat. He was seeking out a Widecombe man for some misdemeanour, hitched his horse to a pinnacle of the church while he threw his victim from the tower and then he overthrew the pinnacle into the church as he loosed his horse again. An explanation like this is much easier to understand than any electrical theory that physics can produce! The moralists made the most of the disaster. The village schoolmaster composed a commemorative poem of considerable length which is now inscribed on boards hanging in the church. It conveys, despite some rather incomprehensible passages, the message 'be good or else . . .' The Puritans incorporated the incident in a cautionary pamphlet which was illustrated with a crude drawing of the packed church and falling masonry. The drawing may have been primitive but I reckon it was based upon an accurate weather observation by someone who was outside the church at the time. Behind the church tower is pictured a funnel cloud hanging from the sky, undoubtedly a tornado. If the artist allowed himself a demon face and fiery tongue to the cloud, who shall blame him?

4

Now the great winds shoreward blow . . . .

Matthew Arnold

Although depressions prefer taking routes north of the British Isles, there are plenty which take more southerly tracks, across England or northern France, bringing the country into airstreams from easterly directions.

Any of these can brew up to gale force and the fact that wind changes direction as a depression centre passes by brings a serious hazard for ships at sea. Although ships can bend before a gale to break its sting and need worry little

Too small a distance between a ship and a lee shore is the nightmare of every sailor. The onshore wind was still driving this wrecked ship, *Hansy,* harder on the the rocks on 3 November 1912. The crew were rescued by coastguards operating breeches buoy apparatus and by the life boats. *(Royal National Life-boat Institution)*

about barriers to *windward* which confuse or accentuate wind, their nightmare is to be blown on to shores to *leeward*. The trouble is that as every depression centre passes by, a safe windward shore can become a perilous leeward shore, which is why Britain's coasts have been littered with more wrecks like the *Hansy* (p29) than will ever scatter the offshore depths.

The shipwreck problem was one which exercised Admiral Fitzroy when he became Chief Meteorologist to the Board of Trade in 1854. The grand title did not imply anything like as much knowledge as a similar post would imply to-day because meteorology was still in its infancy. But the admiral knew as much as anyone, having been at sea since he was a youth and having amassed a fund of weather information which he wrote into his *Weather Book*. Even the revised version of this in 1863, however, showed that there were crucial gaps in the theories he tried to evolve from his observations. For instance, although he was a fervent believer in the barometer as a forecasting instrument, he only mentions the isobar once in his book, and then in a muddled statement about magnetic currents. He sometimes implied that wind causes change in atmospheric pressure, rather than the other way about, and he seemed unaware that all winds, not only those of intense tropical storms, blow in concentric circulations. Nevertheless, as Chief Meteorologist he advanced the cause of meteorology enormously by devising the storm warning system by north and south cones for display at coastguard stations; by starting a system of collecting regular weather observations and plotting them on maps, and through his campaigning for greater use of barometers, particularly on ships. He devised rules connecting

pressure changes with anticipated weather and the 'Admiral's Remarks' were often inscribed on barometer cases. Many were correct and helpful, others were only half truths and, I suspect, could have been dangerously misleading.

Royal Charter storm 25 October 1859

By interpreting Fitzroy's weather data for 25 October 1859 into modern idiom, we know that there was a depression off the north-west coast of France in the early morning. It must have been fairly innocuous because no ships plying the south-west approaches reported anything in the nature of a storm during the previous day or night. A cold northerly airstream was blowing down the west of the British Isles while a contrasting warm southerly airstream from Portugal enveloped northern France and the eastern half of the British Isles. These two opposing airstreams infused new life into the depression whose centre deepened fast while moving northeast at about 14mph. Pressure fell rapidly in southern England, about 11 mbs in six hours, and by late morning SE gales were blowing in the English Channel. Admiral Eliot, whose squadron was in the neighbourhood of the Eddystone Rock, was having a rough time, but at 3pm the wind ceased, the barometer steadied at its lowest level of 28.5in (965 mbs) and the sun shone even though the sea continued to build up. Within half an hour the respite was over, the barometer started to rise as rapidly as it had previously fallen and for the next few hours wind blew with hurricane force from the opposite direction, NW. These dramatically changing conditions must have marked the centre of the depression which then continued northeastward to impose the same tumultuous wind pattern over England and Wales.

In the Irish Sea the *Royal Charter*, a vessel of 2,719 tons with both steam and sail power, was making a passage from Ireland to Liverpool, the last leg of her journey from Australia. At first she experienced a light E wind since she was well to the north of the advancing depression, but as the centre got closer the wind backed to ENE and then to NE and increased in speed. By 3am on 26 October the *Royal Charter* was off the north coast of Anglesey, near Moelfre, gale winds were blowing onshore and she ran aground and was held fast. Wind increased to hurricane force and backed further to N as the depression moved onwards. About 7am this iron ship was totally destroyed within an hour and the captain and 400 of the 430 persons aboard were drowned. The enquiry which was held could establish no particular cause for the tragedy. The ship had excellent instruments on board, including a barometer, her steam engines were running at the time she struck, her sails appeared to be in working order. Sensible estimates of wind speeds that night varied between 60mph and 100mph but the higher speeds seemed to have been south of the centre where the forward movement of the whole storm augmented the winds circulating round it. At Liverpool, for instance, the storm was never excessive, and though there were many other wrecks that night plenty of vessels less sturdy than the *Royal Charter* weathered it safely. Fitzroy claimed that if the *Royal Charter* had made a starboard tack earlier in the night she would have been well clear of the coastline.

With hindsight it was easy to say that that would have been a prudent tactic, but I am suspicious that it could have been the admiral's own Barometer Remarks which persuaded the captain to do just the opposite. Pressure was falling fast and he would rightly have relied on the rules that 'a rapid fall indicates wind' and 'a fall of half a tenth of an inch is a sure sign of storm'. But there was another maxim which stated that 'the barometer is generally lower with wind from the SW and higher with wind from the NE', and the captain would certainly have noticed the sky clouding over from the south. He could have made an erroneous deduction that wind was therefore about to change to the SW which would have ensured him offshore wind and a little protection when close to Moelfre. What he probably did not realise was that it was a whole depression advancing from the southwest, and that his position relative to the centre was going to be crucial for local wind direction.

The importance of this shows up best if we draw maps of the *Royal Charter* storm in the way a modern seaman could with the benefit of radio. He would draw the first chart from pressure readings and wind data broadcast in the shipping bulletin, and he would draw the others as projections in time estimated according to speeds and direction of travel given in the General Synopsis. A vessel near the Isle of Wight, say, would then know enough to expect wind direction to veer (change in a clockwise direction) from S-SW-NW, while a ship near Anglesey would anticipate the wind direction to back (in an anticlockwise direction) from E-NE-N.

If indeed the captain of the *Royal Charter* did wrongly anticipate the direction in which wind was going to change, and therefore sought shelter from a shore which he thought would be to windward but in fact proved to be to leeward, it was an ironical tragedy. The depression was one of the fiercer varieties which bear much similarity to proper hurricanes and a

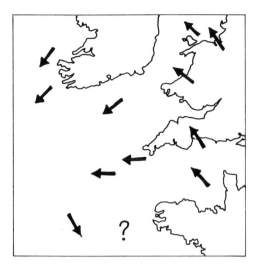

0600 GMT 25 October. Wind directions raise suspicion of depression in north of Bay of Biscay.

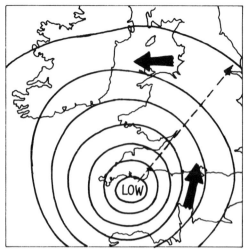

1800 GMT 25 October. Depression fully developed and plotted from information in shipping bulletin

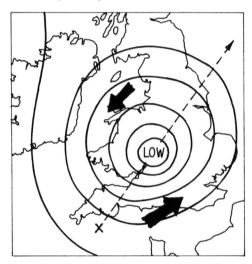

0001 GMT 26 October. *Anticipated* situation based on speed and direction of movement given in earlier bulletin. Wind on south coast expected to have veered, wind over Anglesey expected to have backed

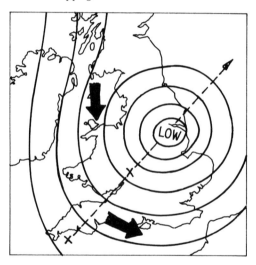

0600 GMT 26 October. *Anticipated* situation showing wind still further veered on south coast but still further backed over Anglesey

The *Royal Charter* storm of 25-6 October 1859, as might be experienced and predicted by a modern seaman with the benefit of radio shipping bulletins.

man of the captain's experience in sailing both hemispheres must have known all about the violent wind changes in tropical storms. Had he treated the depression with the same caution as he would a proper hurricane he might have allowed himself more sea room and sufficient time.

32

The Great Storm 26-27 November 1703

There have been so many storms which have been given the title 'The Great Storm' by the people who have written about them after suffering the shock of their impact that it is hard to know which really deserves the title most. A candidate for the dubious honour of the worst depression Britain has known is that of 26-7 November 1703. (In the modern dating system this would have been 6-7 December for a new calendar was adopted in 1752 and eleven days were omitted that year between 2-14 September to get matters straight.) There were no official statistics of weather then but Daniel Defoe was living in London at the time and recounted the disastrous storm for posterity. He advertised for reports about the storm but was meticulous in discarding any which could not be authenticated or which smacked of exaggeration.

It had been windy everywhere since the middle of November and already a Russian fleet of 100 vessels near the east coast had been dispersed in a gale, some reaching safety at Newcastle or Hull but many others foundering. All the harbours and ports were crammed with vessels prudently awaiting better weather. Outside the harbours many more were lying at anchor: twenty laden ships from the West Indies at Bristol, several fleets of merchantmen in Plymouth Sound, Falmouth, Milford Haven and Yarmouth Roads. There were also 106 merchant ships anchored in the Downs, the sea area between the east coast of Kent and the Goodwin Sands. As well as merchant ships there were many naval vessels, for Britain was engaged against the French in the War of the Spanish Succession. Outward bound for Lisbon to help the King of Spain three fleets of ships with troops from Ireland were waiting off Portsmouth and Cowes, with attendant storeships and merchantmen wanting the benefit of the convoy; a mixed fleet of British and Dutch naval ships were anchored off Holland, and an assorted collection of men-of-war and supply ships were in the Thames. Moreover, a large fleet of warships had just arrived back from the summer campaign in the Mediterranean and were anxiously waiting to dock. They were cumbersome with heavy armaments and wanted wind from astern or on the beam to manoeuvre in restricted water. Admiral Sir Cloudesley Shovell's flagship was anchored off Harwich with most of the larger ships, waiting to make Chatham by the main channel from the northeast along the Essex coast, and the others were anchored with the merchantmen in the Downs. Never before could anyone remember such a concentration of shipping along the coast of southern England.

On Friday, 26 November, pressure fell rapidly during the day and strong SSW winds increased to gale force over southern England by the afternoon and increased in violence after dark. The storm reached its peak in the West Country about midnight. The Eddystone lighthouse disappeared without trace with all its occupants, including its designer Winstanley who happened to be visiting at the time. The furious wind drove water up the Severn valley and flooded a wide area, causing thousands of sheep and cattle to be drowned. Bristol had 8ft more water in the town than had ever been recorded previously and vast damage was done to goods from the West Indies and America which were stored in the warehouses. Everywhere haystacks and trees were blown down, church roofs stripped of lead and steeples toppled.

In London and the south-eastern

33

counties, the storm increased between 2am and 5am and then remained at a peak till about 6.30am. Defoe was living in a well built brick house but his chimney stack collapsed and he fully expected his house to follow suit. However, he thought burial indoors preferable to risking escape to the garden, because nothing was safe within 200 yards of any building owing to flying tiles, which were digging up to 8in into the ground. One woman who opened her door to try to escape thought better of it but was then unable to shut the door against the wind which continued to blow into her house for the rest of the night. After 6.30am the wind started to subside and by 8am Londoners dared go outside, to find the streets littered with wreckage, roofs off everywhere and many houses destroyed.

The Thames was a shambles, with something like 700 ships blown together into the river bend at Limehouse, the wildness of the wind having been accentuated by a high spring tide at 4am which deprived vessels of shelter even from the banks.

Offshore from Harwich, Admiral Shovell's warships had taken down their yards and topmasts but, finding that they could not beat the storm, they raised anchor and let the wind take them into the open sea, most eventually finding safe refuge in Holland and the flagship *Association* in Gothenburg, Sweden.

In the Downs, ships were less lucky. The wind at peak strength was blowing from WSW and certainly well above hurricane strength of 74 mph. Some ships sank at their moorings, a few suffered broken masts only but the great majority dragged their vital anchors and were blown remorselessly towards the Goodwins. The smallest ships were able to float over the Sands because of the high tide but the larger merchantships and warships stuck fast.

The nightmare scene was described in a letter from a merchant seaman, J. Adams, whose ship narrowly missed collision with a warship drifting helplessly to the sand bank. All its masts were gone, the decks were often completely underwater from the breaking seas and the men aboard were in confusion and despair. Their cries, mingling with the firing of guns every half minute in a vain call for help, left Adams 'half dead with the horror of it'. His own vessel fired no distress signals because it was obvious no help was possible. They put out two anchors and cut down their masts in order to ride easier, but when one anchor gave way about 6am they realised their only hope was to try for the open sea before being driven too far to leeward. Rigging an old tarpaulin as a mizzen sail to give some steerage, they edged out of the Downs close enough to the Goodwins to see ships being pounded to pieces, and reached the open water of the North Sea. They saw other boats drifting in the same condition but were helpless to offer any assistance, and reached Norway safely on the following Tuesday.

By daylight twelve men-of-war were seen wrecked on the Goodwins and by midmorning they had broken to pieces with the loss of over 1500 lives. Further along the coast the warships *Resolution* and *Newcastle* had been dragged over shoals but had managed to beach near Selsey. Hundreds of merchant ships were sunk and in harbours ships were tossed together like discarded toys. As many as 8000 lives were estimated lost at sea that night, including those off Holland. Over 2000 of these were naval men; they were considered to have lost their lives in action, and at Queen Anne's suggestion their relatives were assisted out of public funds. The blow to British naval power can be gauged from the fact that afterwards prisoners of war and even convicted prisoners were persuaded to join the navy in exchange for their freedom.

On land, about 125 deaths resulted from the storm and the damage done, nearly all south of the river Trent, was enormous; 100 churches were stripped of lead, 400 windmills overturned and 800 houses blown down. One town in Norfolk, unnamed, was almost destroyed by fire because no one could approach the first outbreak for fear of being blown into it and no one could get near enough to leeward owing to the heat.

All normal business stopped while people tried to get order out of chaos. Bricklayers and tilers entered a golden age of soaring wages for their valued services but tiles became scarce and rose 500 per cent in price — beyond the purses of many people, who used wood instead. Many of the storm-felled trees went straight into use as repair timber. Farmers for about 25 miles inland were bothered with windborne salt which made fields unsuitable for grazing, and many wheat stacks had been entirely shredded by the wind.

A gentleman in Oxfordshire saw, during the afternoon of 26 November, 'a spout marching with wind like the trunk of an elephant, which snapped the body of an oak, sucked up water from cart ruts, tumbled an old barn and twisted its thatch in the air.' It seems certain, therefore, that there were tornadoes in the forward quarter of the depression and it was probably these which lifted wheat-stacks bodily and set them down elsewhere intact. Farmers salvaged these by threshing right away, as much for the demand for thatching straw as for the wheat. Paradoxically, there was a glut of wheat on the market after the storm for this reason and prices fell.

Defoe toured London to inspect the damage, which was obviously similar to that of modern disasters, with thousands of falling chimneys doing the most harm. Buildings on London Bridge, despite the fact that they were high, exposed and not very strongly built, had not suffered greatly. Defoe's explanation, apologetically given because he did not feel qualified to express an opinion, was that the arches beneath had relieved the pressure of wind on the houses — to which we might add that the bridge had benefited by not having the aggravation of other buildings close by. Defoe also noticed that houses which were aligned north to south were stripped on the east side (leeward) but often undamaged on the west side (windward), while low leeward buildings suffered more than higher windward ones. Had builders taken more notice of his observations the aerodynamical behaviour of wind over roofs might have been understood much earlier!

It would be nice to turn up an official weather chart of that storm, but none exists. However, it is possible, from what reports are available, to make a reasonable supposition about the situation. Defoe owned a barometer but did not read it that night, partly because he was too worried about the house collapsing and partly because the readings had already fallen so low that he thought children might have been interfering with it. That could have been the case, because pressure valves at Upminster sent to Defoe later by the Rev W. Derham, FRS, revealed nothing which has not happened many times since. The lowest value was 28.72in (973 mbs) just after midnight and it remained there till about 6am when it rose hastily again. If we plot all the values he took on to a barograph chart (p36), two distinct rates of fall and rise in pressure are evident.

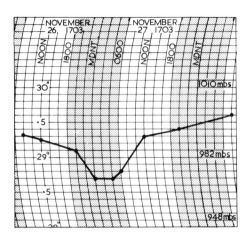

Pressure as recorded by the Rev W. Derham, FRS

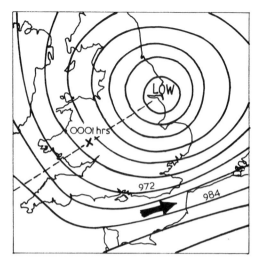

0600 GMT 27 November 1703. Storm at its height near the Goodwin Sands

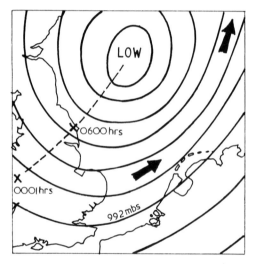

1200 GMT 27 November. Wind eased in London but still from between south and west. Favourable wind in North Sea for fleeing ships

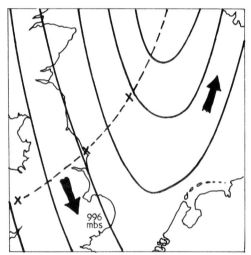

1800 GMT 27 November. Afternoon thunderstorm in London indicates deep northerly air. Wind in North Sea still driving ships to Scandinavia

A reconstruction of the great storm of 1703 from the evidence available.

A depression north of Scotland probably caused the strong SW winds and falling pressure during Friday morning. A second depression, probably crossing the Midlands, could account for the more rapid rate of fall in the evening, with an obstinately resisting anticyclone over France and natural

funnelling effect into the constricting boundaries of the English Channel accentuating wind speeds in the southern half of the circulation.

After daybreak the depression appears to have travelled on a more northerly track, perhaps merging with the earlier depression, because the

36

crippled ships in the eastern North Sea must have had following winds in order to reach Norway and Sweden. Moreover, in London the wind did not veer at once when the barometer started to rise fast, shifting only tentatively towards WNW before backing S again. But by 4pm a strong N wind was blowing and a heavy thunderstorm lasting for quarter of an hour in London indicated that deep cold air had penetrated the country. The charts on page 36 seem consistent with all the known facts.

As for the speed the wind reached that night, the most telling indication is the number of fallen trees, which we can assume to be equally sturdy in every century. Defoe counted 17,000 trees down in Kent alone before he tired of the task. He estimated that elsewhere some 450 parks lost between 200 and 1000 trees each, and the New Forest about 4000. Many of these were really large trees like oaks, elms and beeches, which implies something exceptional in wind strength. The Rev Derham had evolved his own notation of 'storm strength degrees', based on one storm in 1693 which he called 10 and another in 1701 which he valued at 9. His wind vane blew down in the 1703 storm but on evidence collected from people who had actually been outdoors that night he estimated there must have been 15 degrees of storm. Assuming the earlier 9 and 10 degree storms to have been the equivalent of those which produced disaster in Glasgow this century, say 70-80 mph, then that would indicate that the wind speed in the 1703 storm could have reached about 110-120 mph at its peak. This would certainly make the depression something Britain has not seen since, but if it happened once it could happen again. I am coward enough to hope that it won't, but should it do so then modern meteorological resources may help us to understand why such exceptional depressions occur.

5

The rain descended and the floods came

Matthew 7.25

On many of the occasions described so far, cloud and rain accompanied the gales, but the wind was the only contributory factor to the disasters and certainly the only feature which stuck in the memories of the sufferers. But, of course, rain is sometimes disastrous in its own right.

There are two types of rain-bearing cloud. The first type is extensive flat sheet cloud, condensed from warm air which is forced to slither upwards over cooler, heavier air below. The resulting cloud wedge may stretch several hundred miles ahead of the surface boundary between the air masses, called the warm front; the whole cloud formation travels on the horizontal winds of the day, and rain may be light or heavy but is usually continuous for several hours.

In contrast, convection clouds look like billowing cauliflowers and form in strong vertical upcurrents of air. They have a relatively small base area; they may be initiated by thermal activity (see p9) and pass overhead on the horizontal winds as isolated individuals, or they may form in line when an aggressive cold air mass undercuts warm air ahead and forces it to rise and cool abruptly. This is called a cold front. Really deep convection clouds often make up for their brief sojourn overhead by delivering torrential downpours of rain, and perhaps further flaunt their vigour with thunder and lightning.

Anything which accentuates the lifting process may lower the cloud base and intensify rainfall, and therefore mountainous areas always have wetter weather than flat country. But there is a more important lifting mechanism associated with the pressure pattern which finally determines if cloud becomes an efficient rain factory. Surface wind is always backed from the wind direction higher above ground because of friction, which means that, in an anticlockwise circulation, surface air converges towards the centre forcing air aloft to rise upwards to make room. This convergence gives a virtual monopoly of rain production to depressions and troughs of low pressure.

On a weather map, pressure changes smoothly and 'high' and 'low' are relative terms only. There are ridges of high pressure, if only transitory, between depressions of very low value, and there are depressions which nudge their way on to the scene when pressure hugs the top end of the pressure scale. Whatever their actual value, pressure patterns with anticlockwise and convergent winds are troublemakers.

Deep depressions with strong winds, which give dramatic 'catherine wheel' isobars on the charts, often bring heavy rain but travel away quickly before they can create disaster. It is the innocuous-looking troughs with indecisive forward movement which often cause the most trouble because they result in continuous rain over a limited area.

Let me give you some idea of how wet Great Britain is according to standard gauges designed to prevent splashback and loss through evaporation. East Anglia, being flat and furthest away from the advance of the Atlantic depressions, gets about 600 mm a year (24in); the western sea-boards have more like 1200mm a year, and mountainous regions may register nearer 5000mm a year. But on about 90 per cent of all wet days rainfall is less than 5mm (0.2in) and even in the wettest mountains fewer than 5 per cent of rainy days record more than 50mm (2in) in a day. Nevertheless as much as 250mm can fall during one day anywhere in the British Isles and the fact that it occurs very seldom does not make it any better when it does happen.

The problem, of course, is not so much what falls from heaven as what happens to it when it reaches the ground. Nature has carved her own waterways according to average needs, but the efficiency of the drainage system depends a lot on the condition of the soil. An open sandy soil with plenty of space between large particles of eroded rock allows easy percolation of water downward, but a soil as closely textured as clay is difficult to penetrate. Any grade of soil in between these extremes acts as a control valve for the disposal of rain, retaining some for the use of plants and filtering any surplus through to underground streams and thence to rivers. The control function breaks down either when the soil is waterlogged or when it is baked hard, and then rain runs off down any slope available to accumulate as puddles, ponds and floods and fills constricted channels with great rapidity.

Mossdale caving disaster 24 June 1967

June 1967 had been dry and the ground was rock hard when ten pot-holers, mainly members of Leeds University, set out on an expedition into the Mossdale caves near Wharfe-dale in Yorkshire on Saturday, 24 June. The forecast contained the ominous words 'thundery trough' but inevitably memories of rain were blunted after the long spell of dry weather. There were, of course, no signs of unusual water in the caves to give tangible reminder of floods.

After a short time in the caves, four of the party returned to the surface and went home, but the remainder continued to explore below. There was no lookout above ground to give any

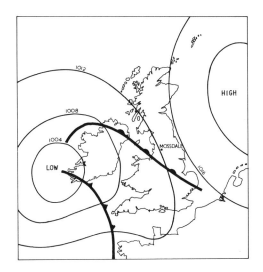

1200 GMT 24 June 1967. Trough of low pressure reactivated an old front to give heavy rain at Mossdale after a prolonged dry spell.

signal that the sky was appearing ominous and when rain started to fall heavily it streamed off the hard ground as if from concrete. Without the controlling mechanism of a porous soil, the underground streams filled rapidly. Inside the caves the water rose at an alarming rate, giving no time for the trapped men to escape, and when none had returned home by 10pm the alarm was given. A rescue party set out for Mossdale and after a perilous crawl for $2\frac{1}{2}$ hours underground they found five bodies huddled together but were unable to get them to the surface then because of the flooding. Further rain hampered rescue work next day but eventually the sixth drowned potholer was found and all the bodies were brought out. It was the worst accident in British caving history.

Norwood sewer flood 7 October 1964

The acres of concrete which cover the soil in urban areas are always impervious to water, so gutters carry rain into drains below ground. They are designed to cope with all rainfalls which can reasonably be expected to occur regularly, but in heavy rain the confined drain channels can fill very rapidly. It is an inviolable rule that a lookout is posted at the entrance when anyone is working on maintenance below.

On the morning of 7 October 1964 there was a depression north of Scotland and troughs of low pressure were swinging round the centre and bringing heavy clouds to the Home Counties. Two men were rebuilding a brick arch not far from the entrance shaft to a sewer in Upper Norwood, London. They had already been called to the surface when rain started earlier but returned again below ground when it stopped.

Shortly afterwards, one of the men came back to the entrance to ask the lookout man to get some wedges required for their work; while he was away on this errand it started to rain hard. The lookout man rushed back and shouted into the entrance but received no reply. Already water was surging through the sewer and when he went down the steps he saw the bodies of the workmen down the tunnel. The fire brigade, who are trained in this sort of rescue work, were called and found the men lying trapped by the open-ended box in which bricks had been lowered down the shaft. The box had floated off its bogey in a rush of water and hurtled down the tunnel to dislodge some timber supports and pin down the two men. There were water marks head high at this point where the water had been temporarily held up by the blockage. The men were unconscious when brought out of the sewer and died before reaching hospital.

This tragedy happened so quickly that statistics of how much rain had fallen would have little significance even if available. The quantity was well within the capacity of the sewer if it had been unobstructed. But the rain fell from a cold front, which typically wasted little time in sprinklings but unleashed its load of water with abruptness. It was unfortunate that the rainwater approached from upstream of the working area and was already building up behind the brick box before it started to rain overhead. Even had the lookout man been at the shaft entrance it might have been too late to get the men back there before the inside dam broke. It is a limitation of the one-man warning system that in built-up areas there is not a wide enough horizon to see approaching rain as is often possible in open country.

Surbiton   6 July 1973

However, few people go down into the drains and above ground, where everyone lives, there is usually room for excessive rain to spread sideways. The risk of drowning is consequently slight, but even small undulations of ground can channel floods into homes when drains are taxed beyond capacity. It happens somewhere in the country every year and even one home flooded is a disaster to the occupant. Since it may be your turn next, perhaps it would be helpful in warding off trouble to examine in detail one small incident.

On 6 July 1973 there was a slack low-pressure trough from Scotland, to south-west England, with cool northerly air behind converging with humid southerly air ahead. It was a classic breeding ground for thunderstorms and Surbiton was the random choice for punishment that day. Rumbling thunder had been

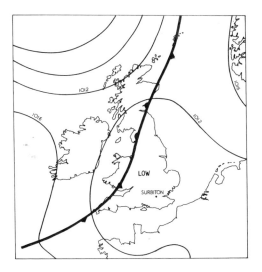

1200 GMT 6 July 1973. Slack low pressure system and old front generates sporadic thunderstorms, exceptionally heavy at Surbiton which had 51mm of rain in 45 minutes and 118mm in 2½ hours. Note the indecisive isobaric pattern, similar to that on the day of the Mossdale flood.

heard since early afternoon but not till 5pm did the grey skies loose their torrential rain, which bucketed down for 45 minutes. Visibility was nil; water drops smacked the earth like heavy sponges and hailstones battered flowers to the ground. Rain penetrated windows and cascaded down walls; terraces became swimming pools and the roads became lakes fed by waterfalls rushing down every sloping surface. A brook, which carries away surface water from the high part of the town and goes under the main road by culvert, became a torrent carrying with it grass and small debris. The culvert entrance is guarded against inquisitive children and large obstacles by a grille which was soon sealed by an impenetrable matting of rubbish. Rain water, denied its proper passage, flooded the playing fields and adjacent gardens, a kind of safety valve operation that has happened before.

Several roads in sensitive flood spots higher up the hill were in serious trouble. People who had been inundated before were dragging their possessions upstairs in helpless anger. They called the fire brigade and about 6pm, when the storm had abated enough to make work possible, the pumps emptied those houses and then did the same for the flooded underpass to try and ease the chaotic rush-hour traffic tangle. All this extra water drained into the brook like a second storm and joined the overland flood near the blocked culvert lower down the hill. There was enough water to fill a small cul-de-sac of houses, not normally subject to flooding, to a depth of 1m. People who had ventured out of doors, confident that the worst was over, found themselves involved in the dreamlike unreality of rescue work. They waded thigh deep in water to contact anxious householders, stumbled against parked cars which bobbed

41

away at their lightest touch and man-handled along the new river boats which had been improbably conjured from landlocked gardens. This was no genteel rowing operation but a tough haul against a fast current, only possible by clutching at every rigid handhold available. Everyone in danger or too frightened to stay in their flooded homes was got to safety, and after the water subsided during the night a dozen homes were left with ruined possessions.

This storm covered an area of only a few square miles, but the resulting floods followed the pattern of every widespread disaster. Inexperienced volunteers carried out the immediate rescue work with whatever apparatus they could lay their hands on; events happened so quickly that no outside organisation could have known about them and provided help in time. It is always thus; people always rise to the occasion and achieve miracles.

By the time the fire brigade were able to start pumping they were still unaware of the overall situation, and this again was inevitable because of the time factor. They quite properly pumped one flooded area without realising they were creating another crisis elsewhere. They could not have known then about the blocked culvert and it would have been unreasonable to waste time making a full survey. Nevertheless, the retention of water by dams of debris is such a persistent feature of flood disasters that some sort of voluntary watch system at strategic points does seem warranted.

Flood water is a filthy, smelly con-coction of mud, debris and backflow from sewers, and clearing it from homes is not within the normal experi-ences of householders. It was as diffi-cult for the few dozen people in Surbiton as it ever is for the hundreds flooded in major disasters. Neighbour-ing volunteers helped next day carry furniture into the streets to dry, to sweep out mud, to lift linoleum and floor boards and to wash walls and furniture with disinfectant. They advised that water should be boiled before drinking and that electricity be turned off; they urged that food-stuffs which could even possibly be contaminated should be thrown away and not put back into the food cup-board. All this was common sense, but more is needed to get a home back to normal. Someone has to pronounce water fit to drink again and that it is safe to turn on electricity—it is too dangerous to leave it to trial and error on the part of the victims. Someone needs authority to provide free disin-fectant and replacement food for those people short of money; someone needs to tap the boundless goodwill of more fortunate people to replace furniture lost by the uninsured, and someone needs to visit the elderly or sick who may be in a state of shock. All this is expert's business and is readily forth-coming on every occasion which popularly rates as a disaster.

The Surbiton storm never rated a mention in the national press; it happened on a Friday and even local people were unaware of the crisis till after the weekend. What the victims and their helpers wanted *immediately*, and did not have, was a well-publicised telephone number by which to sum-mon to the spot a knowledgeable 'disaster officer' to advise, answer questions and take responsibility for those who were too distressed and tired to do anything more. There are good reasons why the community should see that this is the right of even one flood victim.

Heavy rain may be an 'Act of God' but the provision of drains is a job for local authorities; they have an un-enviable job in drawing the line between reasonable facilities to cope with heavy rain which occurs fairly regularly, and unreasonable facilities to cope with any rain which could possibly occur. At Surbiton that day 51mm of rain fell in 45 minutes and 118mm in $2\frac{1}{2}$ hours, an exceptional fall which probably will not occur again in that place for centuries to come. No council could be fairly blamed for not budgeting for that amount of water. Nevertheless, the reasonable calculated risk did not pay off on that occasion and the very best of aftercare for the victims, given quickly, should have been available and would have been a cheap price for the community to pay. Before it happens to you, make sure you can call upon a flood advisory officer as easily as you can call the police or the fire brigade.

Norwich 26 August 1912

Rain belts of longer duration dumping their innocuous sounding millimetres of rain over thousands of acres obviously produce an enormous total bulk of water to be carried away by rivers to the sea. August 1912 had been one of England's unfortunate wet months and by the 26th, a Monday, the soil in East Anglia was already saturated. A slack low-pressure system stretched across the country with three recognisable centres, the most pronounced of which, off the coast of Norfolk, was deepening. Cool easterly air from the North Sea around the northern half of the circulation contrasted markedly with warm westerly air round the southern half. Forecasters recognised the convergence of the two as an obvious rainmaker, but they could not specify the amount, any more than forecasters can today.

It started raining over Norfolk at 4am and by 9am Norwich had recorded 26.2mm. All the county's ditches

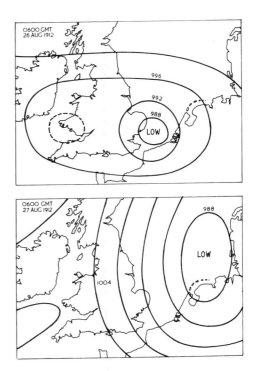

0600 GMT charts for the two days 26 and 27 August 1912, when Norwich was badly flooded, recording 185mm of rain in 29 hours. The offending depression was the most easterly of two apparently innocuous centres in a slack low pressure system extending across southern England, Wales and Ireland.

and rivers were running fast and carrying silt and debris which caused a blockage in Norwich drains and some flooding during the forenoon. Fortunately that trouble was quickly located and cleared and the flooding subsided. It continued to rain all day, often in tropical downpours, and the streets soon ran with water unable to escape down the brimming drains. The north-westerly wind freshened to gale force, whipping surface water to a fury and giving rain drops a vicious malignity. By 6pm Norwich had had 165mm of rain and this figure was increased to 185mm by the time rain ceased at breakfast time on Tuesday, 27 August. This was the equivalent of three times an average month's rainfall in just over a day, and an estimated 671 million tons of water over the county. Standing crops were ruined and stacks sodden through. Broadland had reverted to one large lake and Norwich was cut off from the rest of the country because roads and railways were impassable in all directions.

Approximately one-third of all the rain fell into the catchment area of the rivers Yare and Wensum to the west and north-west of Norwich. On Monday night bridges over the Yare had collapsed on the outskirts of the city, but partial damming of the river was relieved by the sideways spread of water and the area was sparsely populated. The river Wensum, however, passes right through the city centre and, though it kept within bounds during Monday, on Tuesday it could no longer be contained. A torrent of water poured through the town carrying everything from dog kennels to fences. The bridges were at first lined with people watching in awed fascination, but police moved them on when it became evident that the flood had got beyond entertainment level. Street after street became inundated and families were driven upstairs to watch anxiously as water crept nearer the upper floors.

Rescuers in rowing boats were soon out doing what they could but in the swift current even experienced boatmen capsized sometimes. Normal features of the streets became hazardous underwater obstructions; eighteen people in one boat were wrecked on a submerged railing and re-rescued by another passing boat just before their own sank. One hero of the day rescued 100 people in 12 hours' continuous work, an achievement marred only by one tragedy. He came upon a family clinging to a boarded window with only the sill as foothold. The husband had his arm around his wife's waist, the water was nearly up to their necks but both were convinced that they had their two children held safely. Not till the distraught woman was safely in the rescue boat with her three-year-old child did she discover that the baby had disappeared into the water and was never seen again alive.

Prospective mothers had their problems, too, and their gallant knights. A policeman and an MP carried two nurses on their shoulders for 50 metres through water almost up to their necks, and over two brick walls in the process, in order to lift them into the bedroom of a woman in labour. A middle-aged man who had been rescuing people for six hours slipped into the water and was drowned.

There was no possibility of this disaster escaping anyone's notice and all the town rallied to feed the homeless, hand out dry clothes and provide temporary shelter. Corporation carts brought people away from their homes when necessary and delivered emergency rations to those who remained in their upper floors: $\frac{1}{2}$ pint of milk, $\frac{1}{2}$lb of pressed beef, $\frac{3}{4}$lb of chocolate and a 2lb loaf for each person, as well as two candles and a box of matches for each household. About 2500 people were taken into schools, church halls or private homes that day.

Wednesday brought bright sunshine to mock the scene of desolation, and everywhere there was evidence of the destructive power of fast-flowing water. Bridges are always among the first casualties, being built for traffic and not for submersion; fifty-two were destroyed or damaged in the county on this occasion. Paving blocks had been ripped off many roads which were also studded with holes due to subsidence. Every weakness in building foundations had been exploited by the flood. The printing works of the *Norwich Mercury*, on the banks of the river,

44

had a gaping hole in its side and was so badly undermined that it had to be demolished along with several other industrial premises in the area.

In another part of the town, a young woman was in her home when she noticed one of the walls bulge outward. She rushed out to raise the alarm and found the whole back of the house broken away from the rest and several inches out of perpendicular. The woman next door fared worse. She was crossing her landing when the side of the house collapsed; before she could recover from the shock the front wall collapsed as well, leaving the roof miraculously suspended and herself exposed to the world as if in an open doll's house. The whole row of houses had to be evacuated and eventually demolished.

Damage did not always show up at once and there were some nasty surprises in store for those who thought the worst was over when floods started to subside on Wednesday afternoon. Damage to the Ostrich public house had been noticed on Wednesday morning but supports were placed against the building and business was as usual that evening. By Thursday the cracks were more pronounced and the building was cleared of furniture and effects. About 11pm the whole front of the pub collapsed, wrecking a cottage next door but fortunately killing no one.

Although about 3650 buildings were damaged or destroyed—a large proportion of them in the poorer part of the town near the river. If any crumb of comfort could be gleaned from the disaster, it was that it hastened the slum clearance scheme; but this hardly compensated for the immediate problems of workers. Many lost their precious tools in the water, much employment was stopped for a fortnight while industry cleared up the

mess, and 30 shillings from a relief fund was little recompense. This was not yet the era of the welfare state.

The Corporation did considerable improvement work on the river afterwards, because the particularly high level of water in the city was due to the narrowness of the river and its confinement within the built up area. The authorities were spurred on by the fact that there were three mitigating circumstances that day which might not prevail another time: The blocked culverts on Monday forenoon had been discovered and cleared *before* the bulk of the flood water reached the city next day. There was an ebbing sea tide when the maximum amount of water was pouring through the city, thus allowing optimum accommodation for its passage to the sea. And the main axis of the depression, giving the heaviest rain of about 200mm was along a line Brundall to Cromer, which was on the seaward side of Norwich and therefore not inflicted upon it. The worst possible position to be with respect to any rain belt is downstream of its line of approach. The heaviest rain then falls when a torrent is already surging down from the upper reaches. This is what happened at Molesey, Surrey, in September 1968.

River Mole floods 16 September 1968

Friday the 13th is traditionally a day of bad omen and in September 1968 that day held the first seeds of serious flooding in the whole of south-east England. Pressure was highest in the north of the British Isles and the barometer started to fall in the south west. A depression in the Bay of Biscay deepened a little and extended a marked trough of low pressure with convergent airs across northern France towards the Low Countries. An old

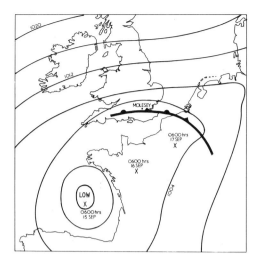

0600 GMT Sunday 15 September 1968. The front across southern England was almost stationary from Saturday, 14 September, when Kent and Essex received the worst rain, until Tuesday, 17 September. During this time the centre of the depression drifted slowly north-east, and south-east England recorded between 150 and 200mm rain in three days. The isobaric chart hardly changed at all and pressure remained constant in the Molesey area.

front became revitalised and swung round the northern part of the circulation to affect south-east England, and Great Britain became totally divided in its weather. Holidaymakers in Scotland enjoyed bright sunshine while England's south coast was afflicted with dismal cloud and rain. The depression was in no hurry to move eastward and the trough remained almost stationary. Kent and Essex bore the brunt of torrential rain on Saturday—Purleigh, in Essex, having just over 50mm in 42 minutes at one time—and by the evening there was flooding in Kent, Sussex and east Surrey.

The river Mole rises in north Sussex and wends a devious route northwards through Surrey to enter the Thames near Hampton Court. It was flowing fast in its upper reaches on Sunday morning when Molesey resi-

dents woke to a steady downpour whose persistent drumming on roof and pavement remained an irritating background to life for the rest of the day. By evening numerous tales were circulating about floods. The Hogsmill at Kingston had inundated several houses; the Mole had topped its banks at Leatherhead and water was over the bonnets of parked cars near the railway bridge. During the night a bridge was swept away at Cobham and by Monday morning an accumulation of water was pressing down river towards Hersham, bursting the banks of the Mole and surging 2m deep under the railway bridge over the road leading to Molesey. The trading estate became knee-high in water, caravans in a nearby field were terrifyingly afloat, houses were awash downstairs and police were trying to get some order into a scene of chaos. Matters had got beyond the scope of self-help and the emergency 'red alert' was given.

Key housewives in the Women's Royal Voluntary Service were told by phone that a rest centre was to be set

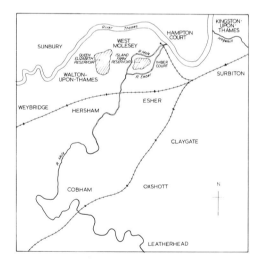

Sketch map of the low lying area around the exit of the river Mole into the river Thames. Some hundred years ago this was a natural flood plain for the river in times of heavy rain.

up in the Playhouse at Walton. They left their household chores unfinished, shut up their homes and while en route made a hasty revision of the principles they had been taught: take names and addresses, help the homeless contact friends, answer queries from worried outsiders, get blankets and mattresses from the council, organise toilet facilities, supply hot drinks using minimum facilities and paying maximum attention to hygiene and where necessary distribute hot meals which would arrive in labelled insulated containers.

Practice, of course, proved somewhat different from theory. No volunteers helping with the endless cups of tea had their fingernails inspected for cleanliness or were forbidden to use over-damp tea towels; the one telephone box in the Playhouse was soon jammed with coins and people had to look elsewhere in order to contact friends; insulated food containers arrived without labels and had to suffer heat loss when opened to discover their contents; boxes taken out to hungry police helping in the flood area were carefully stacked in the horizontal but eagerly grabbed on arrival by one end only. The resulting mixture of stew, vegetables, sponge pudding and custard was unconventional but none the less appreciated!

The crucial thing was that the system worked. About 250 people passed through the centre that day, properly using it only for rest while they organised themselves for the night elsewhere. They arrived by their own cars or by lorries after rescue by boat, but they all had had time to dress and pack essentials into suitcases first. On the whole, they were not in a state of shock and for many the greatest worry was the fate of the animals they had left behind in cages on high shelves.

After flood water had found its level, this main street in West Molesey in September 1968 became a placid navigable river. *(Surrey Comet)*

But all this was still upstream of Molesey, where the Mole enters the Thames. The area is flat, with nearby Esher boasting the only appreciable hill, and the towering sides of two artificial reservoirs being the only other dominant feature. The Mole divides round one reservoir, the eastern stream taking the name of Ember, and the two rivers converge at a common entrance to the Thames.

Molesey business people set off as usual for work on Monday morning. It was still raining and housewives anxious to go shopping saw little to encourage them. Water was running down the roads and the quantity grew alarmingly during the morning. Drains were brimming over and bubbling back into the roads, giving some people an early warning of dangers to come. They acted with unbeknown strength to lift carpets and drag them upstairs and to manoeuvre furniture as well till the top floors looked like furniture repositories. Those who were too fastidious — extracting each carpet tack separately instead of ripping them ruthlessly out — paid the penalty of finding their other carpets already sodden by water coming in through ventilation bricks and too heavy to move. What could not be moved upstairs was lifted as high as possible — tables on bricks, chairs on tables and one three-piece suite survived the ordeal snugly shod in a dozen large bottling jars.

But slight undulations of ground made all the difference between people who could make a controlled retreat from a shallower influx of water and their neighbours whose front paths sloped down a metre from the road. One woman watched the water turn the corner and pour down towards her house like an evil thing from science fiction. She got a carpet and oak chest halfway upstairs, by which time the water had filled her low lying garden to windowsill level and was flowing so fast that debris was breaking the window panes. She bowed to the inevitable and opened the doors, so that the filthy water rushed in at the front and out at the back carrying away many small possessions for ever. It was three days before the water drained away and she could return to shovel the pungent mud from her house, and for six months she and her husband had to live upstairs.

By the time the unsuspecting business people arrived back in the evening, the twists of the Mole and the Ember were obliterated by the impatient water seeking the Thames. Cars were abandoned, traffic was at a standstill and police were quite unable to determine a clear route out of the town. Boats were plying the roads, business people paddled home with shoes and socks in pockets and at least one man, complete with bowler hat, umbrella and briefcase, had his pin-striped trousers draped round his neck. Their first job on getting home was to organise the means of getting a hot meal if the electricity was off. Boxed-in fireplaces were torn open again and coal borrowed from neighbours, or the garden barbecue was rigged up over wet floorboards. One couple lived for three days off the remains of a fortunately overstocked party they had given on Sunday evening.

Meanwhile, a cohesive rescue and salvage operation was being organised from Imber Court, the recreational sports centre for the Metropolitan Police and training establishment for the mounted force. Normally the clatter of horses' hooves, predominance of T-shirts and breeches, and the display of flowers outside the office are more reminiscent of a country estate than a police establishment.

48

This Monday it adopted a more custodial role. The premises and car park were a fortunate dry oasis just above flood level. Old people were brought here by DUKWs or lorries and some spent the night comfortably in clean horse blankets. Women police cooked endless meals, the telephone was constantly in use requesting supplies, answering queries, giving and receiving briefings, and gradually the paraphernalia of aftercare was assembled. Sandbags were filled and distributed by lorries; hundreds of gallons of disinfectant as well as plastic rubbish sacks and giant air dryers from the RAF were collected for use as soon as the floods receded.

Most people were too busy that day to worry much about the future, and there were some incongruous incidents to raise a laugh. A garden seat bobbed down one road, drifted into a garden and settled thankfully on to the door-step as if tired after its unexpected journey. A rush of water from a garage door released a writhing serpent into the flood at which onlookers gaped in horror till they recognised it as a more familiar garden hose. Little things like that were welcome distractions from the more frightening rumour that the Queen Elizabeth reservoir, well above adjacent roof tops, had cracked and perhaps was about to burst. The rumour was repeated on a BBC programme without having been confirmed with the Metropolitan Water Board authorities, who alone could have known the truth, and by the time the information had been appreciated as false it was impossible to suppress. Denials by the BBC and by the police at Imber Court did nothing to quell local uneasiness.

On Tuesday the river Wey broke its banks and the Thames overflowed at Sunbury. All down the Thames boats were loosed from their moorings and careered downstream in crazy exhilaration at their new-found freedom. The Mole at Cobham, however, started to subside and during Wednesday the improvement spread downstream. Thursday showed a marked improvement at Molesey and by Friday the Mole was back on course leaving the ghastly aftermath of clearing up.

There was mud, broken glass and debris everywhere. A noisome stench pervaded streets where sodden vegetables and meat were swept out of shops to be collected by the refuse vans which were continuously touring the district. Sacks crammed with spoilt possessions stood forlornly at every gate, waterlogged carpets lay in gardens like beached whales for burning or cleaning. Firemen pumped water from underneath floorboards and paratroopers wielded RAF heaters to speed the drying process. Volunteers scrubbed walls for elderly householders — and firmly resisted the suggestion of doing the same for a small minority of young and able-bodied people who did not relish the idea of scrubbing for themselves; the Red Cross and St John's Ambulance Brigade visited those who might need medical attention and tried to persuade reluctant owners of badly contaminated and sodden upholstery that it should go to the scrap heap. Those who escaped flood damage searched their homes for unwanted furniture, and this formed a stock pile in a local hall on which people could draw.

Gradually an outward appearance of normality was restored but the after effects lingered a long time. The drying machines, which had the greatest success in rooms emptied of furniture, achieved sometimes illusory results. Wood appeared dry on the surface but was still permeated with water. Fires and radiators, burning all day to dry out homes, created just the moist tropical atmosphere conducive to fungus growth; if it was washed away with bleach one day, it was back again the next. One couple, who left radiators on and windows closed against burglars while they took a recuperative holiday, had to scrape away from walls mould like stinking, rotten cheese when they returned. Everyone complained of stench and endured bare floorboards for months.

Psychologically, many suffered for a long time. Two elderly ladies forsook their home near the river for the lesser evil of a high rise flat, others adopted the practice of taking treasured possessions upstairs to bed every night. Many had their fears revived several years later when they were woken in the night by a flood warning alert. Some still cannot leave home in wet weather without making constant phone calls home to check that all is well. Gardens have never been the same; lawns are overrun with moss, and flower beds choked with hitherto unknown weeds whose seeds were brought down from other areas or uncovered from soil depths by scouring water.

Inevitably there were recriminations and attempts to apportion blame. The Meteorological Office was criticised for failing to give any warning of the amount of rain expected — an unrealistic demand in the light of present knowledge. Timing the departure of a depression which is in dilly-dallying mood is as difficult as timing a snail crossing a road. Clouds are a factory for continuous rain production and radar can only capture an impression at one moment of time, not the total end product. This particular depression did not drift to the Low Countries till Tuesday 17 September, and then only after a last spiteful outbreak of rain in Kent. In the three worst days, parts of Surrey, Kent and Sussex

recorded between 150mm and 200mm of rain, and since this spread round the north part of the depression on an easterly wind drift its impact upon the Mole was the worst possible — from the source to the mouth. In addition, there had already been about 50 per cent more rain than usual in the Thames basin between April and September, so that a low absorption capacity of the soil was possibly as pertinent a cause of the floods as the actual rainfall itself.

The local authority was criticised for having failed to provide a satisfactory flood prevention scheme, because the Mole and the Ember had burst their banks before. A two-year improvement scheme, started in 1955, was put to the test in 1960 during very heavy rain when both rivers coped without overflowing. The scheme appeared to have been an adequate compromise between the possible and the impossible, but the disheartening thing is that any scheme can so quickly become out of date as new building projects anywhere upstream cause quicker runoff of rain from still more acres of impervious concrete. Moreover, the very presence of buildings at all in the low-lying area surrounding the Mole's exit to the Thames is the real risk; 100 years ago the Thames, Mole and Ember wandered at will during flood times over what was then marshland; the present suburban sprawl is a trespasser on a natural flood plain.

The Thames Conservancy was criticised because it had been slow in taking flood precautions and opening all the sluices on the Mole that Sunday morning. The success of the earlier prevention scheme depended upon the mouth of the Mole being kept clear to prevent a build-up of water in the upper reaches, but if a sluice is shut when it should be open it loses the right to that technical name and really

50

becomes a blockage. There does seem to have been inadequate communication between weirs that day and a suspicion that the weekend rota of inspectors was inadequate. The snag is that the weather does not defer to holidays and curiously even seems to prefer them for its more dastardly actions.

The Government came under fire, too — money being one of the major worries. Insurance companies were on the spot at once assessing claims for their clients, but many people were not insured and the local authorities incurred enormous expenses. An MP demanded that the Government should pay; but the Government hedged, saying that it had never been its policy to make direct grants to flood victims. A Minister flew over the area to assess damage but was 'very cagey about grants'; relief funds were opened in different boroughs but had varied success which seemed to relate more to the press and television coverage than to the actual needs of the areas. No adequate funds were available to meet the claims pouring in to the local authorities and by the middle of October the Government was forced to agree to help but still did not quantify the amount. By that time the familiar feeling of neglect had reached a pitch which exploded into wrathful marches of protest when the Minister of Housing stated that he did not think a public enquiry into the disaster would serve any useful purpose. His opinion could well have been right but it was hardly a tactful reply to people who had suffered through no fault of their own.

In the resentful atmosphere which prevailed, people even criticised the magnificent initial rescue operations, and hankered after the Civil Defence force which had been disbanded. There were renewed calls for establishing a National Disaster Force although it is doubtful if any national body could have done better during the first emergency because they could not have been physically assembled and transported to the area as quickly as was needed. However, the work of the voluntary organisations during that initial period would probably have benefited by having one controller with complete direction over the whole flooded area. Imber Court performed this function for Molesey but many rescuers outside that area professed no knowledge of any directing body at all. More practical than a National Disaster Force would seem to be a well-trained Local Disaster Officer, able to contact all the organisations which already exist and co-ordinate all resources and efforts so that there is no overlapping. The scope should include aftercare, because leaflets with instructions are no substitute in dire crises for human contacts.

A £2 million scheme of flood prevention works was compiled after the 1968 floods and has since meandered through the usual hazards of public objections, counterproposals and indecisions. By 1974 a scheme was approved for rebuilding the banks of the Mole at its junction with the Thames, for straightening a stretch of river and building a new relief channel. Work begins early in 1977, nine years after the disastrous flood. It is understandable that local people are apprehensive that remedial measures may be too late to avert further catastrophe. Molesey people, however, can console themselves that one natural feature makes them better off than many others. There are no immediate steep slopes and deep watercourses down which water loaded with debris can accelerate to become a demolition sledgehammer.

6

What a dreadful noise of water in mine ears . . . .

William Shakespeare

When an already potent mixture of low pressure and contrasting, convergent airs meets high ground, the effects can be drastic. Not only does the additional lift of air traversing the obstacle result in more rain but the rapid tumble downhill between steep banks gives water a lethal power.

South-east Scotland   12 August 1948
Just below the neck of Scotland lies the collar of the Southern Uplands, the Moorfoot Hills and (nearest the North Sea) the Lammermuir Hills. The latter rise over 500 metres in places and are drained by an intricate web of small rivers which fall from the north face to the valley of the Scottish river Tyne and from the south face to the Tweed valley. The first week of August 1948 was wet in this area and a further belt of rain spread across south-east Scotland on 11 August from a depression moving east from the Bristol Channel. By breakfast time on 12 August the depression was squatting over Norfolk with an elongated trough extending to Tweedside, where the ground was saturated. An ESE wind was renewing the trough with moist air off the North Sea and the extra lift of air over the Lammermuir Hills resulted in torrential rain all day. By evening, water was cascading down the slopes and along the rivers, bringing down boulders from the treeless heights and uprooting trees and bushes in the valleys.

The significant intrusion of man into this mountainous region has been the building of roads and railways, utilising wherever possible the easy topography of river valleys. In particular, the valley of the river Eye takes the railway line northwards from Berwick-on-Tweed to Dunbar. The curve of the railway line has been smoothed as much as possible and the twisting river runs beneath bridges alternately on one side of the track then the other. By the evening of 12 August the arches of both road and rail bridges were jamming with debris and holding back water as lakes. One by one the bridges were underscoured and collapsed. The released water hurtled downwards, carrying dam debris, broken stonework and brick, and boulders up to 5 tons in weight. Other bridges downstream collapsed like skittles under the assault.

By next morning the transport system of the area was a shambles. Seven main line railway bridges over the river Eye had been destroyed, together with several road bridges and the pillar of a viaduct near Eymouth. Five major bridges over the Blackadder and most of those over the

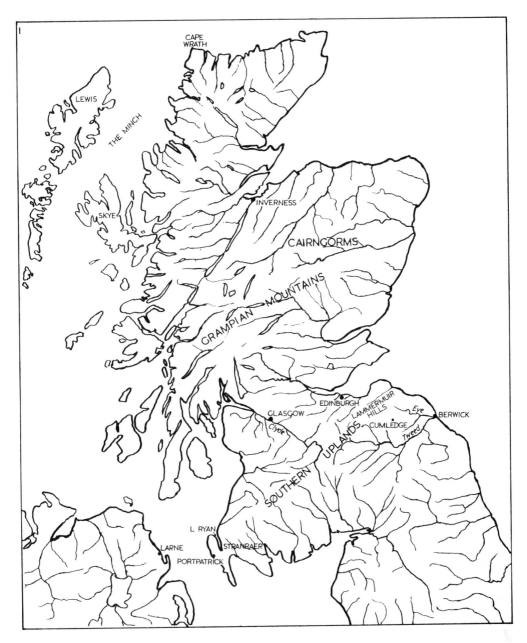

Scotland and its rivers — indicating the scenes of
disasters mentioned in this book.

Whitadder were damaged or destroyed, as well as one important bridge
and several lesser ones over the Tyne
and its tributaries. Landslides further
blocked roads and railways, and soil
was washed from farmland to stain the
sea for 2 miles out from shore. Hundreds of acres of farmland in the valleys
were covered in 2 metres of mud and
boulders, but the region is sparsely
populated and there was little damage
to domestic property and no deaths.

53

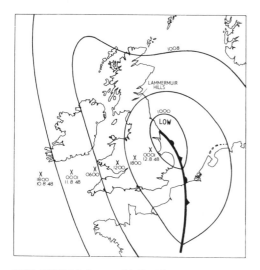

0600 GMT 12 August 1948. The trough of low pressure extending from the depression centre off Lincolnshire, inflowing damp air from the North Sea and the sudden lift of air over the Lammermuir Hills conspired to give 125-150mm of rain in 24 hours in many places in south-east Scotland. These amounts were undoubtedly exceeded up on the mountain heights.

Cars were swept away at Abbey St Bathan and masonry was eroded from a blanket mill at Cumledge. Water swept into the factory, tumbled the great reels of fibre, and matted the bales of cloth with mud, grass and twigs so that the mill appeared to be wrecked for good.

It took months for the area to get back to normal. Engineers from the Department of Scotland helped to clear the fields of boulders and gravel so that crops could be sown next year. River banks were generally rebuilt with grass, which binds the soil well, so long as a watch is kept for burrowing animals. And near the rivers woody bushes and trees liable to break under the strain of rushing water were cut down and replaced by more supple varieties which would bend to any flood.

The Lower Whitadder was so badly

Flood water is a filthy, smelly concoction of mud, debris and backflow from sewers. This was the scene inside the blanket and tweed mill at Cumledge after the floods in south-east Scotland on 12 August 1948. *(Daily Mirror)*

damaged that the whole channel was rebuilt to improve the passage of water, and the same was done in some parts of the upper reaches of the Tyne and above the constricting gorge at Abbey St Bathans. The constriction itself, which could only be altered by blasting operations, was left for a later time, and some of the improvements involved taking the calculated risk of merely pushing the bottlenecks further downstream. Some compromise was essential, as in all similar situations. A completely effective reconstruction would have required unlimited money, a ruthless attitude to property owners and one authority to carry out the whole project — by which time the area would probably not have been worth living in.

Railway bridges were replaced with temporary military bridges and then, gradually, by permanent structures with wider spans and using concrete and steel instead of masonry. It was two months after the flood, however, before trains were running normally because a blocked culvert near Ayton, to the south-west of Eymouth, had caused a large lake to form. It had to be cleared slowly by pumping and delayed repairs to the railway embankment, but this was a small price to pay for the greater blessing that the lake was not formed within banks which burst suddenly.

Nearly 150mm of rain fell in places on Tweedside that day, which is the equivalent of an average month's rain. Sometimes the intensity remained at about 12mm per hour for five hours, and all these figures must have been exceeded up on the heights. It cannot be adequately explained even after the event, but the supply of moist air off a long North Sea track was probably a pertinent factor. The odds against it happening again in the same place are considerable, but there are nevertheless two things which cause uneasiness. In September 1841, soon after the main railway line was opened, one bridge was destroyed and five badly damaged in a storm in this area which makes one wonder if there is some specially dangerous feature of topography to increase the risk of damaging floods. Also the records of flood heights marked on the church at Abbey St Bathans have increased ominously over the years. Between 1875 and 1885 there were three occasions with flood marks about 5ft and two occasions nearly 7ft. In the 1890s one mark stands at 8ft and another at nearly 10ft. There was another mark at 10ft in 1910 but in 1948 the flood mark on the church reached nearly 17ft. Even allowing for the fact that the records are not complete, they do seem to hint at some factor, perhaps soil erosion, together with deforestation on the heights, which is leading to an uncomfortably rapid run-off from the high ground.

Louth   29 May 1920

It is unnecessary to have anything as high as Scottish mountains for water to tumble dangerously. Louth lies about 10 miles from the east coast of Lincolnshire in flat country but with the Lincoln Wolds rising to 120 metres a few miles to the west. Rain from these hills drains partly into the river Lud which is normally about 3 or 4 metres wide and passes straight through Louth.

On 29 May 1920 there was a slack low pressure system centred over Wales, almost stationary and extending with troughs both westward over Ireland and eastward to the North Sea — very like the Norwich flood situation. Light easterly wind was bringing cold air from the sea into Lincolnshire while, converging on the country round the southern half of the

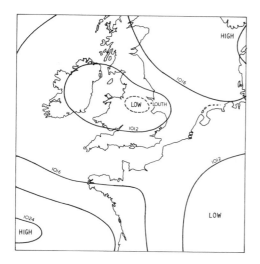

1800 GMT 29 May 1920. The slack low pressure system developed thunderstorms during the afternoon and Louth in Lincolnshire recorded 115mm of rain in 2½ hours. This alone might not have caused trouble, but a dam formed in a valley in the Wolds nearby. Water accumulated till the dam broke and the torrential flood pouring through Louth devastated the town.

trough, was warm moist air from the continent and from the Atlantic. The forecast predicted thunderstorms in many places and Louth was destined to be one of them.

By midday there were thick banks of cloud over Lincolnshire; by 2pm it was raining heavily and was so dark that lamps had to be lit. By 3.30pm rain was falling too fast for gutters to accommodate it, water was coming into windows everywhere and the upper reaches of the Lud and its tributary streams were overflowing into some of the villages.

The river in Louth rose rapidly, 2 metres in ten minutes at one stage, but it appeared to be flowing under control. Those who had to be out in the streets found life uncomfortably wet but the majority of householders turned their attention to the more cosy attraction of Sunday tea.

Suddenly there was a deafening roar

and a torrent of water 200 metres wide swept through the town with absolutely no warning. Frightened faces appeared at windows and stared in disbelief at what they saw. Half a ton of coping stone from the first bridge in the town was lifted 6m into the air, then the bridge crumbled to feed further ammunition into the water. Carriages were tossed aside like playthings and a 1½ ton tar sprayer was lifted bodily over other debris. Many of those who were in the street had little time to notice details like this but were carried headlong into the flood without time for evasive action. Those indoors who were quick witted enough to forsee the outcome fled upstairs where they watched as their chickens, sheds and bicycles were swept away, and the water rose higher and higher.

In some places the river rose 5 metres smashing windows and forcing open doors so that even quick thinking availed nothing. One man stared aghast from his top window, powerless to help as his neighbour drowned before his eyes. Another managed to get the door ajar against the pressing water only to have it slammed back upon his foot by a contrary flow of water from the other side of the house. He had to stay where he was, held fast by the door as the water rose slowly up to his chin before miraculously starting to subside. Another family was so quickly overwhelmed that the only possibility of escape was to climb on to the top of the kitchen dresser. Here the mother clung with her three children, praying in vain for help before the water engulfed them. She had to watch as one by one her children drowned in their own home.

The flood subsided almost as fast as it had risen, leaving one half of the town isolated from the other to make rescue work even more difficult. All six bridges in the town were destroyed, fifty houses collapsed and the fire station was demolished. Seven hundred more houses were damaged and nearly 1000 people were made homeless. Many of these were already the poorest and least able to afford the loss of household goods and small livestock. Twenty-two people were drowned.

Everyone rallied to help. Tents were assembled as temporary homes, the army helped clear the devastated town, Cambridge students arrived in numbers to assist householders. There was plenty for the newspapers to report, not only the inescapable tragic facts but also many popular theories about the cause of the disaster.

Though the rainfall had been very high, 115mm in $2\frac{1}{2}$ hours, the Lud should have been able to carry it. But the flood spread with such rapidity and was of such magnitude that many people said it could only have been caused by 'a water spout in the wolds', which was a misunderstanding of terms. A water spout forms over the sea and is the equivalent of a tornado over land. It has the same funnel cloud, often denser and better defined because of the water sucked up from the surface of the sea; although it occurs near heavy showers it is nevertheless not an open tap pouring water from the sky. There probably were tornadoes that day even though no particularly violent wind reports were received, because at the coroner's inquest one witness described a 'huge cloud shaped like an egg, twisting round and round. Then three distinct flashes of lightning. One of them shot through the cloud and immediately the cloud seemed to come earthwards'. When asked if water was then seen to fall, he said 'it was sheer mist'.

'A cloudburst' was the popular consensus of opinion at first, with the vague implication that the cloud had split in two and emptied its contents like a broken bucket. It doesn't happen like that, of course; there certainly was a bucket which split, but it was earthbound. A bridge near Little Welton to the west of Louth had become dammed by debris and held back water which for a short time filled a valley to a depth of 10 metres. The dam eventually collapsed under the strain and it was this torrent of several million tons of water, released suddenly, which caused the disaster in the town. No one will ever know what innocuous object started the initial dam, but it is a sobering thought that it could have been an old bedstead discarded into the river by some unthinking person too lazy to arrange for its proper disposal.

Devon and Somerset floods
10 July 1968

The south-west counties of England seem to suffer more than their fair share of floods. The boot-shaped peninsula, which is the first port of call for many regenerated depressions from the south Atlantic, is bountifully endowed with high moors and hills to intensify rain. Moreover, almost any wind direction brings moist surface air. Despite the rainfall, however, weather is consistently mild so that the region is much favoured for living in. Small steep rivers tumble down to coastal plains which are densely populated, and it is this factor which often turns simple bad weather into human disaster.

Consider, for instance, an innocuous depression in the Bay of Biscay on 10 July 1968 which decided the time had come to move on north-eastwards. It intensified and crossed the south-west counties across Dartmoor, over the Quantocks and the north Blackdown Hills, and thence over the Mendips.

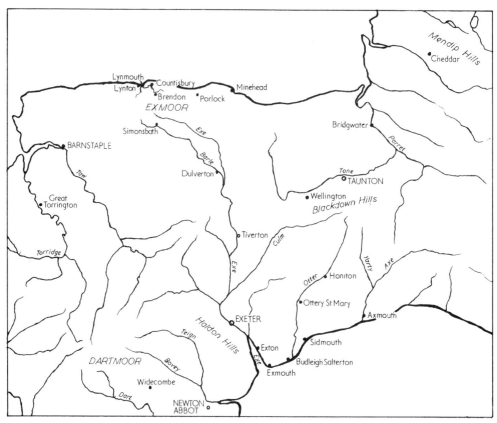

South-west England, most favoured in climate but seemingly prone to disasters because of its high ground and plentiful supply of warm moist airstreams.

At its centre there was a band of particularly heavy rain about 10 miles wide and some places lying within this track received about 125mm of rain in 90 minutes. Somerset and Devon were running with water by the evening.

The river Otter runs down from the Blackdown Hills and was soon over-flowing its banks. Hay had just been cut and was lying in the fields, and the flood water carried it along to pack against the hedgerows till they became impermeable to water. Water built up in dams till the pressure tore up the hedges, roads filled like ditches and every bridge over the river was dam-aged or destroyed. When a command-ing officer came to visit a camp of army territorials next day, there was no one there to be inspected: they were

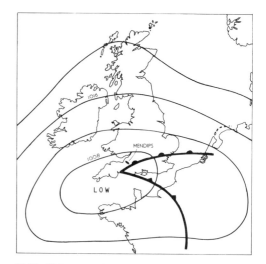

1800 GMT 10 July 1968. The depression had moved north-eastwards from the Bay of Biscay and rainfall was accentuated by high ground in south-west England. Many places recorded 125mm in 90 minutes.

Bridges are built to withstand traffic and not the suction from underneath of a fast flowing flood. Every bridge over the river Otter was damaged or destroyed during floods on 12 July 1968, and next day there was just enough room for one man to edge cautiously across this bridge. *(K. Sansom)*

At the height of any flood, water may flow fast enough to become unnavigable. Above, rescuers struggle in the rushing water after their dinghy capsized during the West Country floods of 12 July 1968. *(The Sun)*

out doing a 'real job' erecting temporary bridges. But there was no loss of life in this valley and damage to property was minimal because the river has a wide flood plain and buildings have generally kept a discreet distance from it. The Otter enters the sea through a tidal estuary and Budleigh Salterton has been wisely built to the west of the river mouth.

It was lucky that this depression merely passed across the upper reaches of the Otter rather than travelling down its whole length, otherwise the tale might have been worse. As it was, the smaller river Sid which follows a parallel course 3 miles to the east and drains the hills which were further removed from the heaviest rain belt, suffered disproportionately because of local geography. The Sid falls between steep sides, increases to a speed of about 10mph in times of flood, has a narrow flood plain and travels right through Sidmouth to reach the sea. There is no widening tidal estuary there; it falls into the sea as if from a drain pipe, over an embankment of stones built up by the tides. There was only one thing the flood water could do that 10 July and that was to overflow directly into Sidmouth, where several people were drowned and much damage done to property.

Meanwhile, it had been raining hard over the Mendips since late afternoon. Between 6pm and 8pm rain often fell at the rate of 50mm per hour and the ground, already wet from previous days, was soon awash. From a distance the Mendips look like ordinary English hills, rising fairly suddenly from surrounding flat country to 250-300 metres. A minor road up the north side is signposted to Cheddar and winds through country which is only remarkable for a few rocky outcrops on the grass verges. Then the road descends steeply — and suddenly,

round the corner, you are in the Gorge. The surprise is breathtaking. The hills open up as if cleft by an axe, the sheer vertical faces of rock are clad in ivy with only small bushes and trees gaining a foothold. Out of season the silence can be felt, accentuated by the echo of even a normal speaking voice and the eerie cries of small birds wheeling overhead. From the plateau above, small tracks wind down the cliff faces, ready gutters for rainwater and pieces of broken rock.

Within the hills there is a labyrinth of underground streams and at some time in prehistory a major water course flowed close to the present entrance to Cheddar village at the bottom of the Gorge. One torrential storm in the past, or perhaps the persistence of many storms, must have altered the labyrinth so that the river now runs 20 metres below its original course. Goughs Cave remains at road level as a big tourist attraction, a fairy land of stalactites and stalagmites, with a scalloped roof which can only have been moulded by the continual pressure of river water. Today the only connection between cave and river is the shaft which acts as safety valve in time of flood and allows water to well up into the cave.

Goughs Cave had been closed to visitors during the afternoon of 10 July and by 9 pm there was so much water from the upwelling stream inside and the rain outside that the restaurant beside the entrance to the cave was also flooded and the occupants driven out. At about 10pm the rain eased and became intermittent; the people of Cheddar mopped up what water was necessary and went to bed believing the worst was over.

At the top of the Gorge a minor road leads to Charterhouse and crosses by embankment a shallow valley full of curious hollows, which indicate collapsed entrances to old lead mines dating back to Roman times. The day's rain had built up into an enormous pond retained by the road embankment; by 2am on 11 July it could take the strain no longer. Water burst through, took the quickest route downhill, over the lip of the Gorge cliffs and into the road just above the entrance to the village. The Gorge cliffs on the other side of the road cushioned the initial impact of the mud and debris, which then followed the road to fill the village in a disgusting but nevertheless fairly orderly manner. No houses collapsed and because no one was outdoors at that time of night no lives were lost, but it took months to clear up the mess. When the road embankment was rebuilt, a large open-ended drain pipe was inserted in the hope of preventing ponding again. This will require a vigilant watch during periods of heavy rain in case it becomes blocked and unable to achieve its purpose.

Lynmouth   15 August 1952

So far all the floods that I have recounted have had some mitigating factors without which the disasters could have been worse. It is very hard to find any redeeming feature about the events of August 1952 which caused the very name of Lynmouth to become synonymous with a flood catastrophe.

The small town on the north coast of Devon has its back right up against the heights of Exmoor, which rise about 500 metres above sea level in places. The road out of Lynmouth towards the east climbs up Countisbury Hill at the frightening gradient of 1:4; while the road towards the west climbs only slightly less steeply, at a rate of 1:6. This latter road passes through Lynton, 180 metres immediately above Lynmouth, and then on past Parra-

combe towards Barnstaple. The rolling moors above Lynton and Lynmouth are drained down the north side by a network of streams which feed into the East Lyn and the West Lyn. These two rivers tumble from the heights between steep sides over stones and boulders to meet in the middle of Lynmouth for their last few hundred metres to the sea.

In August 1952 the hotels of this thriving holiday resort were full with about 700 visitors. The weather had been unkind and the first fortnight had already produced about 115mm of rain, an average quota for the whole month. Exmoor was so sodden that even walking was not an attractive alternative to the sunbathing which people had hoped for. Holidaymakers whiled away the time over coffee in the busy cafés and wandered the streets to imbibe the picturesque atmosphere, hunt for souvenirs and to gaze mesmerised into the chattering rivers. Some of the houses actually overhung the river through the town, emphasising how pleasant was the proximity of water.

On 14 August a small depression in the Bay of Biscay deepened and drifted north-east, giving a new lease of life to a front along the north coast of France. Rain reached Plymouth on the morning of the 15th and spread into north Devon, where it rained continuously for the rest of the day. Cold moist air off the Bristol Channel and the abrupt lift of air over Exmoor boosted rainfall to torrential intensity, particularly between 3.30 and 5.30pm and again between 6.30 and 10.30pm. There was much thunder and lightning; menacing clouds brought unusual darkening and colour effects to the sky, and cloud base over the hills was often so low as to engulf traffic in fog.

The streams on Exmoor were soon

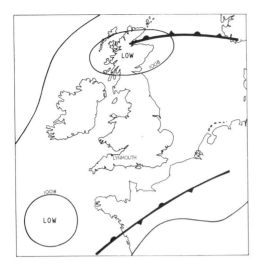

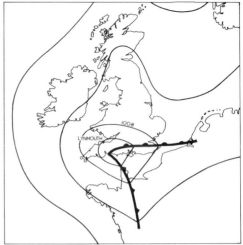

1800 GMT Thursday, 14 August 1952. Low pressure centred over the Bay of Biscay but the English map almost devoid of isobars.

1800 GMT Friday, 15 August 1952. The depression has deepened and moved into south-west England, the old front over northern France had revitalised and the heights of Exmoor accentuated rainfall, recording 386mm in just over 12 hours.

full to the brim, and both the Lyn rivers were running high and fast. However, this was nothing unusual for wet weather and the local inhabitants were not taking much notice though the visitors were fascinated. But even watching churning water can pall in heavy rain and most of them retired indoors, switched on the lights and resigned themselves to yet more reading and parlour games.

On Exmoor a deadly flood pattern was developing. Rivers overflowed or broke their banks, carried with them debris, ponded behind dams in the many hollows of the folding moors or at constricting bridges, and then burst their dams to release suddenly enormous volumes of water. The river Heddon swamped houses in Parracombe at about 9pm, then subsided again till a huge wall of water swept through the village soon after midnight. It broke the bridge, burst open doors of houses and flooded them waist high in a matter of moments, giving

only just enough time for people to get upstairs. One man who went outdoors to give help was unable to withstand the current and was drowned. The river Bray wrought the same destruction as it tumbled down through Challacombe to Brayford and on to Filleigh. Here a party of Boy Scouts were encamped in meadows, wondering why their home town of Manchester should be singled out for jokes about wet weather when Devon could produce rain like that. Some time after midnight, a sudden rush of water swamped the camp and three boys were drowned before they could reach higher ground. At Simonsbath, right at the centre of Exmoor the river Barle flooded houses so quickly and at such depth that there must have been a broken dam to cause it, and further along the moor road at Exford a sudden surge of water flooded a hotel to a depth of 2 metres in a matter of minutes. These rivers all drained down the west or south of Exmoor, but the

62

ugly pattern was also occuring in the tributaries of the two Lyns on the north side.

By 7.30pm Lynton police began to get calls for flood help and realised that something unusual was afoot. A constable and some firemen went to investigate in the area between Barbrook bridge (over the West Lyn) and Hillsford Bridge (over the East Lyn) and found both rivers almost to the top of the bridges. When the men returned from their calls the bridges were covered by rushing water and they just managed to get a warning call through to Lynton before communications went dead. The hydro-electric plant went out of action first and by 9pm the emergency diesel system had also failed. From then on people in Lynton and Lynmouth were on their own in darkness, not knowing what was going on elsewhere and with a perpetual roar of rushing water dominating the night. As the Lyn rivers accelerated down their steep confined valleys they rolled their cargo of boulders and trees as easily as pebbles and matchsticks. The bridges crumbled one by one, water claimed the adjacent roads, and buildings anywhere near became sitting targets every time a dam upstream broke and released its ammunition.

It was a case of everyone for himself and his immediate neighbour. Some who did not get quickly enough to high ground or who were convinced that brick walls were adequate protection paid the ultimate penalty with their lives. Several rows of cottages on the outskirts of the two towns crumbled and disappeared with their occupants, leaving blank spaces near the rivers for incredulous survivors to see next morning.

Down and down rolled the monstrous battering ram towards Lynmouth where the West Lyn rebelled against its traditional route through the town and carved itself an easier path, demolishing everything in its way. The Lyndale Hotel became an island between the two rivers and a buffer against boulders and trees which piled high against its side. By a miracle the building withstood the pressure, but 150 visitors and staff were marooned for the night and had to move from one floor up to the next as water rose and the mountain of rubble grew outside.

In their final headlong rush to the sea through the town the combined rivers demolished the Beach Hotel entirely, pummelled cars into unrecognizable shapes and wrenched boats from their moorings in the small harbour. It was a terrifying night. Police and firemen did what they could to answer cries for help; there were a few dramatic instances of people being snatched from the racing water before they were battered to death, but generally the darkness and strength of current were impossible adversaries.

Rain stopped about 2am on 16 August and soon afterwards the water

The greater the height from which flood water falls and the more loaded with heavy debris, the more powerful does it become. This car was picked up like a child's toy by the torrent through Lynmouth on 15 August 1952 and left as a mass of twisted metal, one wheel completely torn off, at the water's edge when the tide receded. *(Daily Mirror)*

Above:
This was the short cut carved by the West Lyn on 15 August 1952 as it tumbled down the steep heights of Exmoor into Lynmouth. *(Western Morning News)*

Below:
A man gazes incredulously at the size of the boulders carried by the two Lyn rivers and at the destruction they wrought in Lynmouth. *(Daily Mirror)*

started to subside as quickly as it had risen. The outside world had no idea of the scale of the disaster till the same constable who raised the initial alarm managed to drive up Countisbury Hill and over the moors in a wicked mixture of drizzle and fog. He reached Porlock about 4am and alerted everyone to the need for a full emergency operation.

When daylight came, the weary people of Lynmouth found the town more like a battlefield than the picturesque holiday resort they had admired the day before. Streets were impassable, window frames were askew and starred with broken glass, upper floors in damaged houses hung limply as if by one nail and gaping holes yawned in the roads. The sea shore resembled a rubbish tip, frightened animals roamed everywhere and a sad picture of death was developing as one body after another was recovered. It was some days before rescuers finally confirmed a toll of thirty-four lives because bodies were often far removed from the place they drowned or were buried deep in rubble in their own homes. Six of the dead had been visitors (four English and two Australian) and the rest were local people.

The occupants of the Lyndale Hotel climbed out of an upper window on to the boulders outside and picked their way cautiously towards the foot of Lynmouth Hill, the focus for all visitors who were anxious to get away from the nightmare as soon as possible. Some were lucky enough to still have their luggage, others had lost everything, even money. A bus and a van ran a constant shuttle service up the hill to Lynton where rest centres gave temporary shelter and assisted holiday-makers to return home.

There was no such simple solution for the 300-400 people whose homes and livelihood were in Lynmouth —

200,000 tons of boulders obstructed the town and rivers; mud choked homes and shops; water and electricity services were out of action and it was no longer a viable proposition to live there. Some people thought it must be the end of Lynmouth as a holiday resort but they reckoned without the determination of the Lynton and Lynmouth Council and the incoming tide of sympathy and help. Cheques and piggy bank savings poured into the disaster fund from all over the world; parcels of food and clothing arrived so fast that a halt had to be called in a few days; fifty-five caravans were lent and fully equipped with gifts as temporary accommodation for evacuees. Most important of all, workmen and soldiers with emergency lighting, power saws, tractors, pneumatic drills, cranes, excavators and giant bulldozers converged on the town from all over the country. Getting them down the steep slopes into Lynmouth was a remarkable achievement in itself, and in a deafening noise of mechanical activity men worked day and night on an emergency clearance scheme devised by the Council. No one was allowed into the town to hinder the workers, no red tape slowed down any operation and no task proved too difficult. Roads were cleared, temporary bridges erected, river beds unblocked and boulders set aside for repair of the river banks. Temporary repairs were made to the sea wall, unsafe buildings were demolished and broken windows shored up. Over a hundred vehicles in the sea were detected by frogmen and retrieved by the army, no mean feat since the vehicles were often weighted down with rubble. Up on the moors, too, and on outlying farms, the army helped to restore order and get people back into communication with each other. Twenty-eight bridges had been destroyed or badly damaged, 93 houses destroyed or later demolished, 28 cars had been totally wrecked and 38 vehicles disappeared without trace.

Police allowed people back into the town on 2 September; the troops had all left by the 11th and just four weeks after the catastrophe Lynmouth proclaimed itself officially open to visitors again. It was an incredible revival and because of the extraordinarily difficult tasks which were accomplished the operation afforded everyone the satisfaction of a job successfully completed.

The next stage, reconstruction, was not nearly so straightforward because decisions to be made involved supposition and opinion rather than fact. On 15 August, 228mm of rain had fallen in just over 12 hours according to a rain gauge set high on Exmoor near Longstone Barrow. The odds against such a remarkable storm inflicting itself on the same area in the future should be very great — except for the uncomfortable fact that the only two occasions in the records of the British Rainfall Organisation which exceeded this amount were in nearby Somerset. Cannington had 238mm in 24 hours on 18 August 1924 and Bruton had 243mm on 28 June 1917. Three such occurrences in a small area during a relatively short time-span indicate a susceptibility to excessive summer outbreaks of rain which cannot be ignored. A repeat performance had to be catered for, but the problem was how far to sacrifice the charm of Lynmouth, its greatest asset, to considerations of safety. It was no good talking about a voluntary watch to ensure debris did not accumulate, because in rugged country like Exmoor debris is merely a euphemism for trees and huge boulders. No one person, or even several, could hope to clear such obstructions in high-speed tumbling water, even if they were detected.

Admittedly, many of the culprit trees in the 1952 disaster had been blown down in gales during the previous March and the lesson was well rubbed in that never again must fallen trees be left lying near the river longer than necessary. But many others were uprooted by the flood itself and this could happen again in similar circumstances.

Inevitably the first report presented by the Dobbie Committee to the Devon Water Board erred on the side of caution. The proposals for check dams, relief channels, extreme widening of the rivers and bridge spans large enough to allow the passage of all trees, and prohibition of rebuilding on many sites, caused considerable dismay. People felt they would so alter the character of Lynmouth that the vast amount of expenditure required would be counterproductive and the town no longer worth living in. Eventually a lesser alternative was agreed.

The site of the demolished Lyndale Hotel was not redeveloped but turned into an open car park; the West Lyn was channelled into Lynmouth somewhere between its original entry point and the one it had chosen on the night of the disaster, and a new wall was built to separate the outflowing rivers and the small harbour by the shore. Bridges over the rivers were rebuilt a bit higher and with somewhat longer spans, and stretches of both rivers were widened and had some bends and constrictions eased out. In particular, a new road was built to separate the river from restored buildings in the town, and the river was given instead a large bite out of the recreation ground opposite. Also a complete new stretch of road was built at Barbrook in order to re-site the bridge across the West Lyn more advantageously. Special attention was then given to reconstructing the banks of the river to ensure that any boulders or trees in flood water would get a smooth passage down to the sea. The banks were faced smoothly with boulders and through the town itself a flat terrace now joins the top of the cobbled banks and steps to a higher recreation ground. It certainly looks more functional than the old river did, but holidaymakers have taken kindly to the artificial flood plain. It faces south and is an admirable sun trap for lazing in deck chairs. As far as appearances are concerned, the scheme was a great success and the village is still delightfully picturesque. Obviously, people were worried that the lesser scheme might prove inadequate and every wet spell raised anxieties until each passed safely so that the inhabitants relaxed a little more.

Devon and Somerset   Autumn 1960

Probably the most testing time was the autumn of 1960 when Devon suffered heavy rain from several troublemaking depressions in quick succession after a wet summer. Between 28 September and 1 October the Withycombe brook flooded Exmouth, a church collapsed at Exton, the river Torridge rose higher than it did during the 1952 Lynmouth storm and a wall of water caused chaos in Weare Gifford. Axmouth became 'another Lynmouth' when a dam of trees and boulders burst through the town, tearing up the streets and inundating houses. Devon railways suffered enormously during these few days.

Five days later, when Devon was getting on well with mopping-up operations, another depression started to drift up the English Channel. Torrential rain on 6 October renewed flooding; in Exmouth nearly 1000 houses were re-invaded by mud and much equipment used in clearing up

the first flood was lost in the water. The Taw valley flooded, the river Lyn ran high enough to be watched with alarm, and a serious threat developed in the Great Haddon hills. A culvert under the new Exeter-Newton Abbot road became blocked and a huge artificial lake formed, with the road embankment acting as retaining wall. The embankment was still new, unconsolidated and not yet grassed, and it was no laughing matter to have it under pressure from something like 32,000 tons of water. There was the further danger that water would overtop the road and cause dangerous back-scour as it fell over the far side. All traffic was diverted. Inflatable rafts lashed together and to trees, were loaded with portable pumps which the Devon County Fire Service operated all through the night by floodlight. It was still raining when they started to pump and at first the deep lake only fell at a very slow rate. Later the level fell faster, the expelled water had room to spread sideways and did not cause undue impact on any one area; the danger passed safely because of the prompt action taken.

By Saturday, 8 October, yet a third depression with heavy rain reached the south-west from the Azores, bringing the additional discomfort of high wind which raised tide levels and caused flooding at some coastal resorts. This was the day that Exmoor took the brunt of the rain and the flood pattern of 1952 repeated itself. Roadwater, Dulverton, Washford, Porlock and Tiverton had particularly severe floods and Brendon reported a rise in water of 2 metres in 5 minutes, which must have resulted from a broken dam. At Lynmouth, millions of gallons of flood water came down the two rivers again bearing boulders and trees. It was estimated that under former conditions the river level would have

67

risen 6 metres as a result, and disaster would again have befallen the town. As it was the defences held satisfactorily and Lynmouth was confident that it had struck a reasonable balance in making provision against the weather.

Those three depressions, dominating seven days out of ten, were quite enough to designate Devon as a disaster area and a flood relief fund was launched to help the victims. The Mayor of Taunton urged the inhabitants of Somerset to be particularly generous in thankfulness that they had escaped floods themselves, and perhaps this was tempting providence too much. On Friday, 21 October, another depression emerged from the complex low pressure system over the Atlantic and on Saturday it poured with rain and renewed flooding in east Devon—120 houses were inundated at Sidmouth, cottages collapsed at Ottery St Mary and two boys drowned. Bridport in Dorset had water 2 metres deep in places. It rained hard again on Wednesday the 26th and by the next day the rivers were unable to cope. This time Somerset took its punishment. The Tone overflowed into Taunton at breakfast time and rapidly filled the town centre. Vehicles floated away, shop windows were broken and merchandise decorated the waters which cut the town in half. The swollen river Parret combined with an incoming tide to flood Bridgwater; Minehead and Wellington were swamped as well. But once again a Devon town took the worst pummelling. For the fourth time during this relatively short period Exeter was flooded, recording 50mm of rainfall in 24 hours to make a total for October of 386mm, more than half the average annual amount. The Exe burst its banks at lunchtime, flooding 1000 properties and marooning many people in shops and offices where they had to remain for the night, their only contact with the outside world being via messages relayed on the BBC. It was heartbreaking for residents who were just making headway against the filth of earlier floods.

7

Snow on snow, in the bleak mid-winter

Christina Rossetti

Depressions perform their task of condensing water vapour from the air all through the year, but when it is cold enough in winter the end product may be snow rather than rain. This is a regular feature in Europe because large land masses cool rapidly as the sun declines and days shorten, and most wind directions bring cold air. But sea reacts only very slowly to seasonal changes and around Britain the sea temperature never falls much below 5°C away from the shore. It therefore has a warming influence on all airstreams journeying to the British Isles. South-westerly airstreams continue to bring rain all through the winter; northerly airs are usually warm enough near the ground so that snow showers melt soon after falling, except in the mountains, and even bitterly cold easterly airstreams from the heart of the continent, bringing prolonged snow falls, are warmed enough by the short journey across the North Sea to give temperatures only a degree or so below freezing by the time they reach Britain. Air temperatures do fall far below zero centigrade at times, but usually during the fine cloudless nights between snow belts rather than during the snowstorms themselves.

Winter weather, therefore, depends upon the track of depression centres. If they stay mainly north of the British Isles winters are mild and wet, except where latitude or mountain height tip the balance towards snow. But if persistent high pressure elsewhere keeps depressions moving over southern England or northern France, then the whole of Britain comes into the cold continental airstreams which feed the circulation, and hard winters result. It does not, however, happen often enough to encourage people to adapt their lives accordingly.

Snow starts life as tiny hexagonal pieces of ice which feed upon the water vapour in the air and grow symmetrically with spokes, plates, prisms and rods from all six sides. The finished crystals when seen under the microscope are like exquisite diamond brooches. Temperature, humidity, wind and direction of fall determine the final crystal and over 6000 patterns have been discovered, which doesn't pretend to be the limit.

When the crystals are heavy enough they fall to ground, either interlocking as snowflakes or sometimes acquiring additional water which freezes to round them off as pellets. The white cover which first settles on the ground may contain as much as 90 per cent air, but then the crystals react to their new environment and alter shape.

During a blizzard snow may settle sparingly over open country, but it packs down hard in the eddies to the lee of obstructions. In February 1947 this railway cutting near Pontywaun in south Wales had to have a huge cornice sliced away on the side from which the blizzard was blowing, but the far side of the cutting remained fairly free of snow. *(British Rail)*

Some of the tips vapourise and then condense out again as ice over the centres of the crystals so that the shapes become more rounded. They nestle more closely to their neighbours, may even bond together, and the proportion of air in the snow cover drops. When a strong wind blows, snow packs hard against windward obstacles and often shapes into waving cornices in the back eddies of wind to leeward. Cornices may project 2-3 metres outward as self-supporting mouldings over empty air, looking from below like beguiling sculptures but appearing from above deceptively like the snow on solid ground.

Snowdon   15 January 1972
On 15 January 1972, snow was lying on Mount Snowdon where a company of soldiers was on a training exercise on one of the peaks. During the afternoon cloud lowered as a blanketing fog and

it began to snow again. The men lost their way and the lieutenant in charge went to reconnoitre, but when he did not return after two hours the company found their own way down the mountain to raise the alarm. An RAF search party found no sign of the officer, either on the peak or in several gullies, and the Volunteer Search and Dog Rescue Team was called upon. The Alsatian bitch, Elsa, was trained to rescue from avalanches even in the dark, and she and her handler combed the peak in the difficult snow and worked their way round the valley. Elsa tugged to go up one gully already searched by the RAF and, since she remained eager, she was allowed to go free. She started digging far up the gully and the dead officer was found beneath 45cm of hard packed snow, lightly camouflaged on top with fresh snow. He must have walked across a cornice which was indistinguishable from the snow on firm ground and it had broken off under his weight.

Cairngorms   21 November 1971
Snow has even more subtle ways of proving the power behind its simple, beautiful appearance. On Saturday, 20 November 1971, the weather was fine when a party of schoolchildren from Edinburgh and two women teachers left an outdoor education centre near Aviemore with one of the instructors for a climbing expedition in the Cairngorms. The forecast warned that there would be heavy snow and drifting later in the Scottish Highlands, and staff reminded them about this when the party reached the chairlift. However, the instructor felt that no progress could be made unless pupils were sometimes schooled in harsh conditions; they were equipped with spare clothing, plastic sheets and emergency food rations, so they carried on as planned.

1200 GMT 20 November 1971. Fine weather in Scotland but the forecast warned of worsening weather.

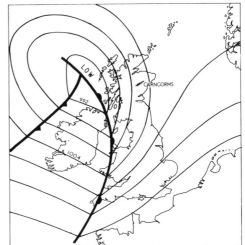

1800 GMT 20 November 1971. Snow blizzard and whiteout conditions in the Cairngorms.

Once up into the heights, the party split into two. The instructor took the strongest children, and the two women the remaining six. The weaker party received no specific directions from the instructor about which route to take or what to do if the weather worsened, and they set off towards Ben Macdui and the Curran bothy—the local name for hut. It was cloudy by now and after they had walked only a short distance it started to snow but they felt fine and continued on their way. The wind increased steadily, snow continued to fall and they were soon enveloped in the classic whiteout conditions of a snow blizzard. The snow was filling every footprint as it was made, and obliterating all the vertical landmarks by which a person usually maintains a sense of balance, while visibility was reduced to almost nothing. This was all the more frightening while daylight lasted because of a natural feeling that one should be able to see. They could not find any cleft in the rocks where they could shelter; there was no convenient hedge to shelter against; they

had only one pair of snow shoes between them, and after three hours of plodding knee deep in soft snow the teachers gave up the idea of reaching the bothy. They realised they must stop the children walking before they got too exhausted. They had no spades to dig snow holes and bare hands were quite inadequate for such a task, but they did their best to cocoon the children under plastic sheets so that the snow would insulate them from the cold. Air temperature was several degrees below zero; most of the children were wearing jeans or needle-cord trousers which were not sufficient to keep them warm, and snow kept blowing in their faces and threatening to suffocate them. Panic set in; some of the children started shouting and screaming, and the teachers had to leave their own snow cocoons to calm them. The women did their very best, but eventually there was nothing left to do except try and get help, and one of the teachers set off.

Meanwhile the instructor's party spent the night in a hut and returned

71

to base on Sunday. The blizzard was still raging and a big search operation was mounted for the missing party. Conditions were atrocious and it was not until Monday morning, nineteen hours after the search began, that the teacher was discovered, alive but frostbitten and just able to say where she had left the others. By the time they were found only one boy was still alive and the other teacher and five children were dead, lying about in the snow as if they had lost all judgement as to remaining still to conserve their strength.

The victims were 1500 metres up the mountain and cloud base everywhere was near the ground. A helicopter managed to find a jutting out ledge where it could set down and take off the boy survivor. The six bodies were taken to the nearby hut and brought down next day when the weather improved. The surviving teacher and boy were carefully nursed in hospital till they recovered and were able to endure the ordeal of giving evidence at the inquest.

It was a sad tale which unfolded. The three adults were all employed either to teach physical education or to organise outdoor activities, their physical fitness and technical qualifications had been adequate for successful expeditions before. The thing that really marked them as amateurs was their lack of respect for the weather.

The instructor was asked if he had not devised some method of toughening children physically before taking them on such a climb; he replied that he thought only adults needed toughening and that children who took part in dancing, games and athletics at school were adequately trained for rock climbing. This ignored the fact that cold weather alone can so alter a person physiologically that fitness becomes irrelevant. The normal behaviour of the human body depends upon chemical constituents — enzymes — which are particularly choosy about the temperature range in which they function. When body heat is lost, skin temperature falls first and when it reaches something like $10°C$ a person loses all sense of touch or pain. If the internal body temperature falls even a few degrees below normal, to about $35°C$, the mind stops functioning properly. Then coma occurs, and death follows when body temperature reaches $26°C$. Even people highly trained in the arts of survival can suffer from exposure without realising it; they stumble, talk incoherently, get outbursts of sudden temper or crazy impulses to curl up on the snow and go to sleep, which they would never entertain if they were in their right minds. The truly competent sportsman, whichever outdoor pursuit he follows, always acknowledges that in certain respects the weather remains master. The alternative to deferring to a forecast of deteriorating weather may be death, and it is against that ultimate penalty that one must weigh up the frustration of a cancelled expedition if the forecast proves wrong.

The evidence of experts at the Cairngorms inquiry was emphatic. In view of the well-known fickleness of weather in the mountains there was a clear risk in such expeditions for children in winter. Remoteness was itself a danger and children should always be within reach of real safety. The huts were merely for emergency refuge and could even be treacherous if they iced up from outside. Many experts felt they performed a disservice by tempting inexperienced people beyond their capabilities. The jury recommended that future expeditions should be led by fully qualified instructors with long experience and that reference should

72

These men were on a four-day survival exercise in the Cairngorms, testing themselves in winter conditions. They were already experienced mountaineers, able to navigate by compass from one map reference to another, suitably dressed against the subfreezing temperatures and equipped to dig snow holes. Just the same whiteout conditions and cold were experienced by the Edinburgh schoolchildren who died in the Cairngorms on 21 November 1971. *(John Cleare)*

always be made to weather forecasts and local conditions.

The Edinburgh Education Committee concurred by proposing higher standards of mountain leadership certificates and stricter medical examinations for pupils at the outdoor centres. During winter all school parties should in future remain within contact of base via staff checks or radio, and there should be no overnight use of any high level shelter or bivouac.

Snowdon 20 February 1972

The Cairngorms inquiry was scarcely over before another accident occurred to some schoolboys from Dulwich College who were walking on Snowdon in Wales. The weather had been generally mild and there was not a lot of snow lying on the heights of the mountain. The trouble was that it had been alternately thawing on mild days and freezing again at night, constitut-

ing a dangerous surface of ice, sometimes camouflaged by fresh snow.

The Snowdon railway is closed to trains during the winter but is a favourite track down the mountain for climbers. It has a gradual slope and this can give a false sense of security. The schoolboys were in good spirits and were indulging in a little 'skating' on their backsides; the master in charge did caution them to be careful about slipperiness but it was in no way a prohibition. Most of the boys tired of the pastime and stopped, but about 15 metres ahead of them three boys slipped, were unable to stop and slid over an unseen precipice 150 metres to their death near a lake below.

It was difficult to attribute blame to anyone in this case. The boys were in no way disorderly, conditions were perfectly feasible for that grade of walk provided one appreciated the slipperiness 'which they all did. Certainly they did not know the local topography well enough to be aware the precipice was there even though they could not have seen it in the poor visibility. Even those who thought it would be safer to close the mountain to walkers in winter admitted that such a measure would be impossible to enforce. One of the officers from the RAF mountain rescue team at Anglesey stated that he had known many accidents at that point of the mountain which is very windswept so that snow packs down hard into ice. He thought a safety fence would be a good idea, and felt it was advisable to rope up and use crampons and ice axe at the dangerous stretch, but he confessed that it was easy to be wise after the event. It was generally felt that this unfortunate episode was an accident in the true sense, an unforeseeable course of events without attributable negligence.

The two winter weather disasters involving children renewed public resentment about the unnecessary risks imposed upon the voluntary rescue services. The increasing number of accidents are not increased by knowledgable or skilled sportsmen — however potentially dangerous their pursuits may be — but by the inexperienced general public who want to join in occasionally and think enthusiasm is a satisfactory substitute for training. Many of them have a wholly unrealistic view of the power of the weather and feel there is something sissy about retreating under its onslaught. Sometimes they do not even give the weather a thought. It is high time that a sensible respect for this potential enemy is inculcated into children before their schooldays are over.

Southern England   March 1891

One of the penalties of lying between such contrasting media as the cold European continent and the warm Atlantic is that temperatures can swing rapidly from one extreme to another

because of a comparatively small difference in depression track. Although December 1890 and January 1891 had been very cold with some of the hardest frost for years, February in England was mild and fine in compensation. Spring flowers bloomed and farmers were well ahead with their sowing. It rained in the first week of March from a depression which travelled north of the British Isles to Norway; it rained again from a secondary depression which formed over Ireland and moved eastward; and on 9 March forecasters suspected a third depression was forming off the west coast of France. They reckoned, however, on high pressure spreading south from Scotland and they forecast, for the 24 hours up to noon on 10 March, fresh or strong easterly winds with fair weather and a possibility of some snow showers in southern England.

In fact, the high pressure was making no headway against the deep-

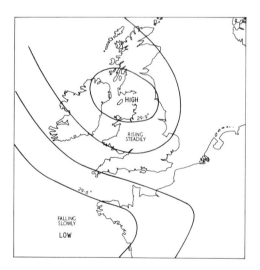

8am 9 March 1891. Forecasters expected the high pressure area to spread southwards giving fresh or strong easterly wind, fair generally but some snow showers, in southern England.

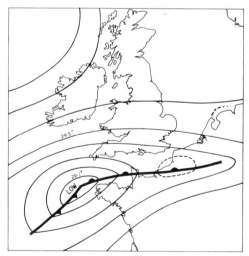

8am 10 March 1891. The Biscay depression deepened rapidly to rout the high pressure. Bitterly cold air from the Low Countries was drawn into the depression circulation and a snow blizzard resulted.

ening depression. There was no radio then to broadcast warning of weather deterioration but anyone in the south of England with an eye on his barometer would have been suspicious of the rapidly falling pressure. A few canny farmers, with a sixth sense about the weather, quickly picked their early spring greens or hurriedly planted potatoes while the thick clouds gathered. By early afternoon on Monday, the 10th, it was snowing over southern England, the deepening depression was moving across France with an elongated trough towards the Low Countries, and by late afternoon gale force winds and blizzard conditions prevailed. Snow was suspended in the driving wind, sweeping over open fields almost without covering them but accumulating in huge drifts near any obstacles. Visibility was reduced to a mere arm's length but it hardly mattered because the snow, having arrived by the shortest sea route, was dry and granular, stinging the face so hard it was impossible to keep the eyes open.

No enemy could have sprung a greater tactical surprise. Ships were at sea without time to make harbour, railways were carrying their normal complement of cargo and passengers and in Devon and Cornwall sheep and cattle were on the moors, too far to be rounded up by nightfall. Darkness added confusion to the storm. Ten trains were stranded in snow drifts but no one knew where because the telegraph lines were down. Horses carrying messengers were soon bogged down and their riders were forced to trudge through the snow if they could, often up to their necks in drifts. Few messages got through and perhaps it was as well, since the inability to do anything constructive to help would have been unbearable if the extent of the problem had been known. None of

the iron ram ploughs could be got to snowed-up trains and the few shovels available were useless. It was hard to see distress signals fired at sea and impossible to launch lifeboats in the high wind. A few lifelines were fired, some exhausted seamen were pulled ashore but, beyond that, all people could do was to huddle inside half buried houses and stranded trains, listening to the demoniacal roar of the storm and the trees crashing all round. It was later estimated that half a million trees had been lost, many of them sturdy varieties like oaks. Sometimes their tops were twisted off or they were felled in narrow swathes between undamaged trees, so there was obviously tornado activity. Almost unbelievably, no one was killed by falling trees though the occupants of one horse-drawn carriage had a remarkable escape when one fell across their path and imprisoned them within its larger branches.

By daylight on Tuesday the shores from Kent to Cornwall were littered with wrecks, fifty-seven around the south-west peninsula alone, and harbours were strewn with broken fishing gear and smashed boats. Thousands of homes were damaged but only a few seriously, and many were snowed up to the eaves. Farmers were desperately worried about their livestock outdoors but there was little they could do because the storm continued all day, exacting further toll on shipping and keeping many passengers imprisoned in trains or railway stations.

By Wednesday morning the depression had moved to the Low Countries and bright sunshine over southern England revealed a fairy-tale landscape under a blue sky. Snow had so altered its contours that familiar territory had become unrecognisable. Thinly scattered snow over a few open fields soon started melting in the sunshine to reveal the dark earth below, but snow drifts filled many roads above their bordering hedges and fences so that people had the greatest difficulty in finding their way about. Snow was even piled indoors, for the driving powder had easily found its way through cracks in doors and windows.

Householders did what they could in the morning to clear snow from their homes. Railway men pitted their puny implements and gruelling efforts in attempts to free the snowbound trains but they achieved little as they sweated in the sunshine beyond releasing passengers. By afternoon another depression approached and the sky clouded over again. Thursday was bitterly cold with gales from the north-east and more snow. Yet another train was trapped and its passengers spent a miserable night in the compartments. The wind abated on Friday though there was some sleet; Saturday dawned wet but cold and then the wind settled into the west; warm air spread over the country again and the thaw started. Spade work was resumed in earnest, main line railways were soon back to normal operation and isolated villages again made contact with the outside world. Farmers who had lifted their vegetables before the storm cornered the market. One man in Lostwithiel who had sown corn beforehand found it had actually germinated under the snow and was 7cm high, others who had planted potatoes had a head start over those who had to delay until the snow melted and the ground had dried out a bit. The daffodil crop in the Scilly Isles was ruined.

Most people caught out in the snow had been able to find shelter before becoming exhausted, so there was little loss of life. One man had a lucky escape when stranded too far from any friendly house. He stood against a hedge, took off his overcoat and put it over his head, kept his feet stamping in the pit he made for his legs and was soon cocooned in his personal cave of snow. Since he took these precautions while he still had body heat to conserve, he survived the night. People stranded in the trains had a thoroughly uncomfortable time but they remained safe during the hours of waiting because snow kept the compartments well insulated against undue heat loss. Sheep, too, being quickly covered with snow and with thick wool to retain body heat, survived in little caves under the snow. Some of the ewes even gave birth to their lambs, to be dug out later by anxious farmers who traced them by translucent patches of damp on the snow surface. But generally, livestock suffered crippling losses. Thousands of cattle and wild ponies were frozen to death and birds were almost wiped out in Devon and Cornwall.

At sea many lives were lost and the tragedy which made the greatest impression in the south-west was the loss of the much vaunted four-masted clipper, *Bay of Panama*. She had been sailing close-hauled along the Cornish coast, taking in more and more sail as the gale increased in fury. Snow and sleet masked any view of the shore but the skipper firmly believed he had enough sea room to allow him to drift back into the Atlantic if necessary. But the wind had been driving him further towards the shore than he realised. About 1am on Tuesday morning the captain noted the ominous short confused sea which characterises shallow water near cliffs. His last rag of sail had blown out; he could not manoeuvre away from danger and the *Bay of Panama* was soon pounded on to the rocks beneath Nare Head. She heeled over towards the sea which poured continually over the deck and into the battered foc's'le where thirteen men had shelter of a kind. Seven others were trapped at the stern and climbed into the rigging to get clear of the sea. They were wet through, air temperature was near freezing level and eventually one man went out of his mind and threw himself into the huge seas despite the efforts of his companions to reason with him. Two more men died during the night and were swinging in macabre fashion from the rigging by morning, but three who had apparently frozen stiff managed to climb down from their precarious perches, eyes closed with salt and ice, every breath an agony.

That sign of life in people thought to be corpses made a great impact upon the coastguards already working hard to effect a rescue of the men who had signalled from the fo'c'sle. They redoubled their efforts and, with great skill and much help to those men who were in too bad shape to do anything for themselves, managed to get all survivors ashore by breeches buoy. The sea was still pounding and the wind blowing a gale; the ship seemed likely to break up as the rescuers looked sadly back at the few dead men left on board. Someone thought he saw one of the crouched bodies on deck make a movement. He wanted to go back to the wreck; a few other rescuers supported his view, but the officers in charge decided a further rescue attempt was no longer practical, nor reasonable in view of the certainty that no one remaining on board had been alive. The niggling doubt of a job not properly finished became a contentious issue with local people and cast an unfortunate slur upon a magnificent rescue. The matter even went before the magistrates but nothing substantial emerged to contradict authoritative evidence that those left

behind were already dead. In the weather conditions prevailing it would have been too easy to imagine a movement on the distant deck, particularly with the fresh memory of apparent corpses getting down from the ratlines earlier and in view of the whole unreality of deaths by freezing in a Cornish spring. It is an ironical fact that only in a normally mild climate with warm flowing seas could this accident have happened. In colder climates ships would have been sealed in behind ice for the winter and seamen would have been ashore instead of afloat.

The forecasters no doubt had some explaining to do about not having anticipated the blizzard, but even today, with greatly increased knowledge and more information radioed from the Atlantic via ships and aircraft, the problem is difficult. A matter of only a degree or two of temperature makes the difference between snow and rain, and a matter of comparatively few miles in the track of a depression makes the vital difference between directions of wind. When a mature depression is tracked across the Atlantic it is relatively easy to anticipate its path across Britain, but the genesis of new depressions on our doorstep is very hard to pinpoint. Shape of isobars gives reasonable warning when a new system is developing, a falling barometer increases the certainty, but just *where* the centre will be and how it will move is hard to predict until the whole system is already causing trouble.

Ross Cleveland   4 February 1968
The particular danger of sudden cold airstreams over still liquid sea is well known to seamen who work the fishing waters between Scotland and Iceland in winter. The land mass to the east and north gets progressively colder

with rise in latitude while the sea remains relatively warm because of the North Atlantic Drift Current. Sudden falls in air temperature to perhaps $-15°C$ or $-20°C$ can occur in the northern part of a depression circulation, and then warm clothing and shelter below decks are of little avail to the trawlermen if the vessels themselves become at risk because of icing.

On the morning of 4 February 1968 a very deep depression was centred just south of Iceland and hurricane easterly winds were flailing the fishing fleet on the western side of the island. Wind and mountainous seas were bad enough but ice accretion in the air temperature of $-11°C$ was much more serious. The upper parts of the ships were as cold as the airstream and the air was full of flying spray which froze on contact with the superstructure. Bridge windows iced up, electrical contacts failed and equipment became

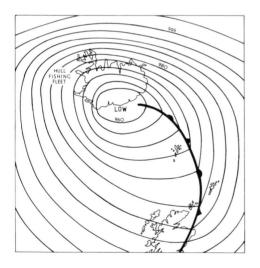

1200 GMT 4 February 1968. A very deep depression south of Iceland brought bitterly cold air, about $-11°C$, to the Hull fishing fleet off the north-west coast of Iceland. Snow and sea spray froze to the superstructures of the trawlers, making them very unstable and causing the *Ross Cleveland* to capsize and sink.

welded to deck in solid ice. It was accumulating at the rate of something like 40 tons in four hours; had it formed on deck only it might have been a safe load, some probably melting in the warmer water continually flushing over the deck. However, the rigging and clutter of equipment above deck level provide endless nooks and crannies in which ice can get a tenacious hold, thus raising the centre of gravity of the ships to make them unstable.

The *Ross Cleveland* and several other Hull trawlers were having a difficult time. Crews were on deck all that Sunday night, hacking ice with axes but it was hopeless trying to keep pace with its formation at low levels and impossible to get at ice higher up where it mattered most. The *Ross Cleveland* was riding low in the water, rolling further and for longer periods, and ploughing deeper with her bows because of the weight of ice forward. The huge areas of ice presented to the wind made it increasingly difficult to hold the ship into the wind and probably the final coup-de-grace was a wave taken broadside.

The *Boston Typhoon*, stranded in Isafjordur harbour, heard a radio message from the *Ross Cleveland's* captain: 'I am going. We are laying over. Help me.' A few moments later came a last message of love to all wives and families. The *Ross Cleveland* lay on her port side, could not be righted and sank in 8 seconds. Two Hull trawlers which had her on their radar screen saw her suddenly vanish. There was no trace of her, no possible chance for any survivors in those seas—just one miracle which raised a lump in the throats of every newspaper reader two days later, the sort of lone survival which encourages every bereaved family to continue hoping long after it is reasonable to do so.

Trawlers fishing in open water of northern latitudes during winter face the risk of very heavy icing when the passage of a depression brings a sudden change to a subfreezing airstream. The *Notts County* was lucky to be safely driven ashore on the north-west coast of Iceland with her load of ice on 4 February 1968; the *Ross Cleveland* capsized and sank because of instability caused by a similar load of ice. *(Topix)*

Harry Eddom was on deck hacking ice when the ship went down and he was swept clear. He blacked out and when he regained consciousness he was in a rubber dinghy with the bosun and another deckhand. All three baled continuously to keep the raft free of water, but the cold eventually killed both of Harry Eddom's rescuers. He himself survived to feel the raft touch bottom, and with what strength he had left he pulled the raft with his two dead companions as high up the shore as he could and staggered inland till he found a house. It was locked and he did not have the strength to break down the door but he knew he would die if he sat down. Sheer will power kept him standing in the lee of the house till day break when a young shepherd found him and led him to shelter and warmth. He recovered in hospital — a miracle survivor from the sea which claims more victims from exposure than it ever does from drowning.

Fifty-nine lives were lost in northern waters (not all because of icing) during the three weeks culminating with the loss of the *Ross Cleveland*, and Hull wives started a campaign to get trawlers banned from Icelandic waters in the winter. It was an understandable but somewhat defeatist view because it denied the very advantage — remaining afloat all the year round — that British fleets have over icelocked countries. Moreover, long-range forecasting cannot predict usefully enough when and where particularly cold outbursts of air will occur, which makes it impossible to define sensibly what the winter 'season' is. In 1927, the much nearer Shetland Isles suffered a severe blizzard which lowered temperatures to $-3°C$ as late as 27 April.

It seems more helpful to learn how to live with icing conditions. After two vessels were lost in similar fashion in 1955, experiments were conducted on models in wind tunnels with subfreezing temperatures, and the nightmare of capsizing vessels was witnessed with horrid reality. Then the equipment on the models was encased in rubber sheathing and inflated from underneath by compressed air after ice had formed. Since ice cannot bend; it simply fell off in chunks wherever the contour to which it had moulded was altered. Halyards were made of hundreds of parallel-laid strands of soft synthetic material enclosed in pliable plastic tubes. It was found that ice could get only a precarious grip on the smooth surface and that smart taps at the base caused ice to drop easily to deck. The equipment was tested in 1969 on a normal fishing trip of the *Boston Phantom* and the research team which went along considered themselves lucky to encounter the weather conditions they were trying to thwart. In a force 10 storm and severe icing, the sheathed foremast stays were kept clear of ice, though traditional metal cables got well coated, and the rubber-panelled front to the bridge was kept ice free. The equipment was judged adequate to allow ships to get to shelter though not enough to allow fishing without thought of weather.

Modern technology, therefore, can do much to beat icing. But is the expense justifiable in view of the infrequency of occurrence? The arguments flow thick and fast every time Britain gets a long and particularly hard winter, and 1962-3 was one of them.

The winter of 1962-3

There had been cold snaps ever since the beginning of December 1962 but on Boxing Day snow fell in earnest from a southerly track depression. By midnight, parked cars in southern England were engulfed in snow and hosts everywhere had to offer overnight hospitality to their guests. It took a few days before all those stranded cars were dug out and then a replica of the 1891 blizzard stranded still more. Snow started to fall on Sunday, 30 December, and continued all day, with winds increasing to gale force and gusts up to 88mph in the West Country. Air temperatures in London and Edinburgh were at freezing level, in Cardiff just below, and even Dublin could muster only 2°C. By the end of the day everywhere south of a line from the Wash to Anglesey was covered in snow. Miles of telephone wires were down, more than 200 main roads were blocked, cars and coaches were stranded everywhere and very few trains were running. There were drifts 5 metres deep in the west, high villages on the moors like Widecombe were cut off completely, and, more unusually, 7 miles of foreshore at Southend were frozen and ice stretched 200 metres out to sea near Shoeburyness.

After the offending depression had passed away there was a feeble attempt at thaw, counteracted almost at once by another depression which brought the rest of the country under the snow blanket that persisted till early March. Week after week the weather charts showed winds blowing 'backwards' across the Atlantic. Scotland, being nearest the dominant high pressure from Scandinavia to Greenland, had a cold winter but with a generous proportion of sunshine. The rest of Britain also had more sun than usual but interrupted by further belts of snow from southerly track depressions. Insult was added to injury when the cold continental air unloaded not only its snow but its dirt as well; bulldozers slicing through drifts in a 3 mile-wide belt inland from Torquay revealed a dirty layer of soot 1 metre above the soil which analysis indicated had come from Stuttgart in Germany.

Remote villages and isolated farmsteads were frequently cut off by snow and when their food stocks ran out the armed forces dug a way through with their heavy equipment or dropped supplies from the air. Feeding the livestock was the greatest problem, especially when they were out on high country like the Devon moors. Cattle will graze through 15cm of snow, but with anything deeper they tend to stand around and look helpless. Anyhow, some of the more lush grasses used in high production farming go slushy under snow and become useless as fodder. Ponies and sheep are a bit more independent and will dig through 60cm of snow when it is newly fallen but 30cm is nearer the limit by the time snow compacts hard down. They manage well on gorse and for this reason no east-facing moor slopes are ever burnt, however overgrown the gorse; snow settles less on the windward slopes than in the fierce eddies down the leeward slopes, and the gorse remains more easily accessible. But nothing helped much in 1963. Once the sheep got into drifts over 60cm and their fleeces were loaded with snow and ice they could not move. Thousands of sheep, ponies and cattle starved to death, huddled together ineffectively for warmth; more died later because their shrunken stomachs could not digest food when it did arrive. Helicopters were invaluable for dropping supplies, but their arrival often posed problems for farmers who had rounded up their animals with great difficulty to a suitable spot. Creatures who normally never batted an eyelid at low-flying aircraft making a full decibel quota of noise often stampeded at the downdraughts from helicopters and were then unable to get back to the rendezvous in their weakened state.

Industry and commerce suffered almost as much as farmers during that winter because of chaotic traffic conditions. Every road journey was an adventure, every commuter train into cities a battle against frozen railway points. Furious arguments developed about the inability of Britain to cope with snow when the continent managed to do so every year, and that was itself part of the answer. Every winter, snow blocks certain European roads and they are simply closed for the duration; while others can be kept open with snow clearing appliances. Such heavy expenditure is therefore an obvious and worthwhile investment, while in Britain, similar equipment would lie idle more years than it would be used.

Moreover, the snow the continent has to deal with is usually very different from the stuff which afflicts Britain. The warming influence of the surrounding seas puts the British Isles into that narrow range of temperatures within which water continually changes its mind about staying liquid or going solid. Snow may leave the continent as dry snow many degrees colder than zero, but when it reaches Britain it is warmer and wetter from its passage across the sea. A mere touch of sunshine after a snowstorm and the surface layer will melt, but a similar touch of freezing again under a clear sky at night will solidify the melt snow to far more dangerous 'black ice'. The name is apt because it cannot be seen on dark surfaces and it causes more road accidents than are ever caused by snow. Sunshine is not needed to melt snow which has a temperature near zero, pressure will do the trick just as well. Hence the main traffic thoroughfares in Britain easily get trodden to a slushy but passable state during the daytime but at the price of more dangerous black ice next night. It would be far simpler, in many ways, if the snow in Britain were so cold that even traffic pressure would not melt it. But it is useless for the British to dream about snow clearing appliances which suck up dry snow and blow it effortlessly away to the side; the machines would simply clog up under the pressure of processing. Wet snow needs the heavy weight of bulldozers.

Nevertheless, the 1963 winter goaded Britain into increasing its stock of heavy snow ploughs at strategic centres, increasing the numbers of heaters on busy railway line points and improving the heating equipment in railway carriages. Until the country becomes so wealthy that it can spend money recklessly there will always be problems. It does not help that forecasters can not predict how often hard winters will occur. All sorts of periodicities have been postulated: a peculiar tendency for odd years to be colder than even, a 12 year cycle of cold winters, an 18 year cycle and the 1963 winter fitted quite neatly into all these categories. Those who therefore bet their money on another cold winter in 1975, specially since the previous three had been mild, were rewarded with a milder winter than has been known since 1869! Had the country invested even more in anti-snow equipment after 1963 there would certainly have been as many grumbles as there will be when the next extreme winter catches everyone on the hop again.

People wanted to know if the first few months of 1963 constituted the 'worst winter ever', a difficult question in view of lack of comparable statistics from far back in history. Particularly low temperatures may occur even in mild winters, usually on nights when still air and cloudless skies permit heat to radiate away from the ground. Obviously, temperatures under such conditions fall even lower when heat loss is imposed on an airstream which is already cold, and in 1963 some stations recorded instances of air temperature as low as $-16^{\circ}C$. On 23 January almost all reporting stations had minimum temperatures below $-10^{\circ}C$ and even the Channel Isles plummeted to $-5^{\circ}C$, which is most unusual. However, mean monthly temperatures are a more significant test of severity of winter and all over Britain these were between $2^{\circ}C$ and $7^{\circ}C$ below normal. Individual stations at Oxford, Plymouth, Edgbaston, Cambridge and Braemar recorded the lowest mean temperatures since they started reporting— which shows that the exceptional cold was equally spread over the country. Kew had a mean temperature for January of $-1.4^{\circ}C$, the lowest since 1838; and for the three months, December 1962-February 1963, the mean was $-0.1^{\circ}C$ compared with

0.9°C in 1947 and 1.0°C in 1891.

As regards persistence of the cold, many places had more than 20 consecutive days with air frost—Harpenden, in Hertfordshire, suffering a startling 36 days—with temperatures often failing to rise above zero all day. Because of this persistent cold with easterly winds, snow remained lying for a very long time, up to 66 days in some places, many of which see no snow at all in most years. Nevertheless, the country succumbed more often to the high pressure influence to the north than to the depression influence to the south, and the winter was drier than usual with considerable sunshine. Snow was not excessive but because the main falls occurred with high winds, drifting caused maximum nuisance and low temperatures ensured that the nuisance remained. The climatologists concluded that the 1962-3 winter was the coldest over England and Wales since 1740, the coldest over Scotland since 1879 and the coldest over northern Ireland since 1895.

As the cold continued in 1963, lakes and rivers froze, and skating became as commonplace in reality as on those nostalgic Christmas cards portraying scenes from the past century. The Thames froze in places and accounts were revived of the last frost fair to be held in London.

London   January 1814

The new year, 1814, commenced in a very dense fog which lasted till 3 January when a southerly track depression deposited heavy snow for 48 hours continuously in north-easterly winds. This was followed by a slight thaw, just enough to make the roads perilous with black ice when air frost gained control again and then continued for 30 days in London. By 30 January, ice-floes which had formed in the upper reaches of the Thames drifted downstream and blocked the river near London Bridge, whose small archways made it more of a barrier than a passageway. The ice floes soon bonded together and on 31 January the first adventurous people crossed the lumpy ice near Queenhithe. By 1 February the river was solid between Blackfriars and Queen St and walking across the river became the chief entertainment in the capital. The small traders grasped the opportunity to the full. They set up canvas booths and sold ginger ale and ginger bread, books, and a great deal of rubbish they could not sell elsewhere, all at exorbitant prices. There were swings and skittles and dancing on a barge; sheep were roasted over coal fires—sixpence to see it done, one shilling to taste a slice! Printing presses turned out commemorative pieces, ranging from the Lord's Prayer to poems about the frost, and the watermen made up for their lack of employment by charging a lucrative threepence as toll to enter this splendid fair. People thronged the river till late at night and it looked very picturesque in the moonlight.

On Saturday, 5 February, the wind shifted to the south, there was a little snow but not enough to detract from the fair and thousands of people trod the central footpath which was still firm and secure. Snow changed to rain in the evening, most people drifted home but some lingered unwisely. There were loud cracks and some printing presses floated away, and two men drifted off on a floe which overturned before help could arrive and they were drowned. A high tide at 2am on Sunday assisted the thaw and by 3am the Thames was alive with crashing icefloes released from bondage. Several more booths were carried away though no more lives were lost, but the jostling ice did untold damage to moored boats. It was a calamitous end

to the last frost fair on the Thames, and there is never likely to be another in London. The reason has nothing to do with caution or the weather, only with the physical change in environment.

London Bridge was pulled down in 1831 and rebuilt to give freer passage to river and tidal water. Marshes were reclaimed at Lambeth and Vauxhall, river banks were built up to allow further building development and the river itself was dredged so that it flowed more powerfully between the smoother boundaries. That all reduced the risk of the river freezing. Then came the power stations in the present century which discharged enough heat into the lower reaches of the Thames to put paid to any idea of a frost fair in London in the future. During the 1962-3 winter, the power station at Kingston-upon-Thames raised the temperature of the river downstream to between 7°C and 10°C even though the temperature at the estuary mouth was nearly 0°C. Half a mile upstream of the power station, however, people walked across the hard-frozen Thames for a few days, so an olde worlde frost fayre might yet be staged one year at Hampton Court.

The two winters 1813-14 and 1962-3 took a heavy toll of human life. This was not uncommon in past centuries while Britain was basically an agricultural and shipping community. The freezing of the ground and the Thames always led to unemployment, high prices and scarce food. Houses often lacked any pretence of efficient insulation and every hard winter resulted in deaths from cold and starvation. It is a sad reflection on the so-called welfare state era that the same thing happened in 1962-3. Hidden within the statistics of specific causes of death lay the undoubted fact that the greatly inflated figures that winter were due to economic factors. When a person gets cold he must stoke up with food, exercise and artificial heat, and the old, the sick and the poor are at a disadvantage in one or all of these factors. Clothing helps to retain body heat which already exists but it does not create new warmth, so that even retiring to bed serves little purpose if one is already too cold for good health. In 1963 the word hypothermia, death by abnormally low temperature, entered forcibly into the layman's vocabulary when it was realised that several thousand people had probably died because they could not afford food or fuel, had no visitors to notice the fact, and were too proud to ask for help.

8

Like an army defeated, the snow hath retreated

William Wordsworth

Hard winters often save their most disastrous acts of sabotage until they are on the way out, and snow is a relentless saboteur. All the time it lies camouflaging the landscape, it may be surreptitiously changing character within. Snow near the ground may vapourise, rise upwards, freeze again on to crystals near the top of the snow and alter their shape to cup-like pebbles which roll over each other and give an unstable base for further snow. At other times a layer of thaw water within the snow acts as a glide for the rest, so that it breaks away as a massive instrument of destruction on to whatever lies below. The worst avalanche disasters in the world happen in mountainous country where villages in the valleys bear the brunt. The mountains of Britain have their share of avalanches but these do not impinge much on populated areas, and the one which still holds pride of place in Guinness Book of Records occurred in the unlikely county of Sussex.

Lewes avalanche   27 December 1836
There must have been a depression over the English Channel or northern France, with freezing easterly wind and a frontal belt swinging round the centre, to fit in with the account now

displayed in Lewes at the Snowdrop Inn — a name which bears no relation to the delightful little flower.

A Mr Thomson set out from London to Lewes at 2pm on Saturday, 24 December 1836. By the time he reached Ashdown Forest, the wind was blowing hard, snow falling heavily and the horses had the greatest difficulty in keeping upright on the indistinct road. Near Lewes there were deep drifts and Thomson did not arrive home till 11pm. As he opened his front door the 'wet' snow which had compacted against it into a solid mass, fell into the house and it was an hour before the door could be shut again.

At the same time, the wind was screaming over the top of Cliffe Hill in the eastern sector of the town. The hill which had been excavated for chalk had a sharp drop of 100 metres to where a row of houses stood. At the edge of this precipice, the wind was slamming backwards in a fierce eddy and gradually sculpturing a cornice of snow. By daylight on Christmas morning, snow had stopped though it was still very cold, and the residents of the houses were studying the giant wave of snow, frozen to immobility, which held tons and tons of snow poised just overhead. Some people from the local authority saw the phenomenon as well, but no one seemed to think there was any risk. On Boxing Day a mass of snow fell into an adjacent timber yard and the owner warned the occupants of the other houses about possible danger to themselves but they shrugged it off.

Now, the one thing a cornice of snow is least likely to do is melt, drip by drip, till it fades away, but perhaps it is understandable that the people of Lewes had not the experience to appreciate the fact. On Tuesday morning there was bright sunshine and about 9.30am a young man noticed that the overhanging snow was intersected with fissures. He ran to the passageway between the buildings and implored everyone to leave but they refused, saying they had nowhere to go. The young man decided it was time to think of himself and he ran clear. Almost immediately part of the huge cornice fell, struck the houses at their base, exploded like a bomb under compression of the air pockets between the snow crystals, lifted the houses bodily off the ground and down again, and when the mist settled all that could be seen was a mound of snow.

Someone rushed to Thomson and 'offered him his purse' for rescue work which he organised with great efficiency, getting shovels from the local ironmonger, directing a gang of men to use them and coping with that age-old problem, spectators whose ghoulish interest threatened to impede rescue. Snow and the remains of the houses were spread right across the road to the high flint wall bordering the River Ouse. The men broke down part of the wall and started to shovel towards the river, but then reconsidered and shovelled back underneath the still overhanging part of the cornice, presumably to cushion the impact of the inevitable next fall.

By 4pm fourteen of the fifteen people buried had been extricated; the remaining one was known to be alive because of his groans. An urgent signal was received from the hill top to run clear because the rest of the snow was about to fall. After it had settled the last boy was dug out, alive but injured. Eight people were killed; the victims are buried at South Malling Church where a plaque records 'the awful instance of the uncertainty of human life'. The tragedy could more properly be attributed to ignorance, because it is inconceivable that anyone acquainted with snow and its behaviour would have remained in those houses to court death.

Glazed frost   January 1940
The release from a hard winter rarely comes via sunshine, because a warm cloudless day is usually followed by a cold clear night. It needs a steady invasion of warm southwesterly air, with all the usual implications of cloud and rain, before grass and earth reappear through melted snow. Unpleasant things can happen in the meantime, and one of the nastiest is glazed frost.

The first winter, 1939-40, of the war was cold and snowy. Since the middle of December there had been frequent easterly winds, much air frost and considerable snow, and by the end of January the ground was rock hard and white with hoar frost and snow. The Thames was frozen for 8 miles between Teddington and Sunbury; there was ice a third of a metre thick on reservoirs near London; the sea was frozen in many places along the east and south coasts; towns and villages had been cut off for days and ice floes created arctic scenes on many rivers.

The newspapers summarised the weather on 29 January, a respectable period after the cold spell really started to bite and by which time people were only too uncomfortably aware of conditions anyhow. Weather in wartime was secret news for fifteen days after the events because of Britain's favoured position on the doorstep of eastbound depressions from the Atlantic. Ironically, everything so far that winter had come from Europe anyhow but the enemy was probably watching for a clue that the situation was to change.

With disarming frankness, the newspapers on 30 January reported that the previous day had been one of complete traffic chaos — few cars on the road, no traffic possible uphill, trains lost in the north and 600 passengers stranded for whom accommodation had to be found locally and cattle slaughtered to feed them. It sounded like a repeat of the past few weeks, and there was no word about the real cause of the trouble — glazed frost. A warm front had inched its way eastwards against

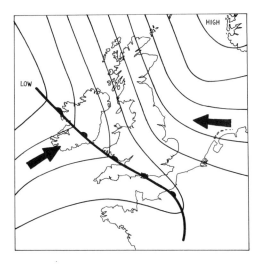

1200 GMT 27 January 1940. A warm front had nosed its way into south-west Ireland and England, and high cloud ahead of it was giving some rain. The surface airstream was still from the Continent and subfreezing. High pressure refused to concede way to the depression and stalemate lasted for three days.

the obstructing high pressure on the continent, managed to spread its canopy of cloud over the country and had then stuck, forbidden by the high pressure to advance further. Snow and sleet fell over eastern England and much of the Midlands, but in Wales and the south of England, the intruding sliver of warm air from the Atlantic produced rain. It fell on to a landscape which was still engulfed in subfreezing air, and the rain solidified to ice over everything it touched. Grass and shrubs looked like artistic arrangements of glass rods, and tawdry metal rubbish turned into sculptures of elegance when encased in ice. Branches of supple trees bent to the ground under their burden of ice and then became welded into position, but many mature trees were felled completely or split down the middle as the ice accumulated unevenly on the windward sides. Telegraph wires, coated on the upper surface, rotated under the weight to present another side to the rain, till huge collars of ice hung from them. Sometimes these were incongrously adorned with upward pointing icicles formed earlier in the downward position. Gradually telegraph poles and wires collapsed; in Gloucestershire, where practically every pole was down, it was calculated — by weighing sections of ice — that 23 wires between two posts carried $11\frac{1}{4}$ tons of ice! Car doors froze solid, railway points were immovable and roads were like skating rinks. Ponies on Plynlimon in Wales were frozen to death in sheaths of ice; birds became welded to the ground or were killed in flight by solidifying wings; and even sheep, which had enough wool and warmth to survive beneath their armour of ice, had to be broken free from the ground. The noise of cracking ice under foot and the tinkling sound of glazed twigs in the wind

When rain falls from a wedge of warm air aloft on to a surface which still has a temperature below freezing level, it freezes to ice on contact. There were three days of such glazed frost in February 1940 and telegraph wires all over the south-west of England were torn down by the weight of ice collars which formed over them. Compare with the huge ice collars on the rigging of the *Notts County*, page 79.

frightened the animals still further.

Glazed frost occurs fairly often as a thawing airstream approaches but it usually lasts only a short time until the warm air penetrates to the ground. In 1940 all the pressure symptoms and wind directions indicated a normal progress of the front, and when that did not happen, the resurgence of the high pressure should at any rate have caused the frontal cloud and rain to disperse. Forecasters were unable to explain the stalemate which lasted till 3 February when another depression asserted itself to spread a proper thaw. Such a long period of glazed frost has

not happened since, and perhaps it was a pity the information did not leak out to the enemy in the first place. It might have confused them as much as the British!

As the full thaw spread across the country, warm air cooled over the snow to give temporary fog, while rivers flooded under the sudden release of melted snow. Cold house walls streamed with condensation, furniture in unheated rooms bloomed over with moisture, and burst pipes sprang to life as gushing waterfalls. Plumbers were kept busy for months, and the additional tasks of removing fallen trees and repairing telegraph lines were jobs which wartime Britain could well have done without. In the long term, the winter impressed two salutary facts on the consciousness of the public. Since the country could not depend upon every winter being mild, it was madness to run unlagged water pipes on the outsides of house walls; and it was sensible and healthy comfort to have central heating like the continental countries had had for a long time.

River Till flood   16 January 1841

Snow is merely solid water stockpiled in a natural refrigerator. After a snowy winter there will be far more water to dispose of than ever falls from one severe rain storm. In regularly cold countries, river beds appear ridiculously empty during the summer months but justify their size in the spring by carrying away melted water without hazard to the countryside. British rivers are carved for a more consistent flow of water, and though some dry out in the upper reaches during periods of dry weather they become grossly overburdened in times of snow thaw.

In 1840 there had been a long

period of frost and snow in southern England before Christmas and the cold returned again in the first week of 1841 after a brief thaw. Snow was lying thickly on Salisbury Plain on 16 January when high pressure retreated to admit warm air on the south side of a vigorous Atlantic depression. Temperature rose rapidly to around 5°C, heavy rain fell, which always speeds up snow thaw, but the ground was still hard frozen beneath the snow and unable to assist in disposing of melt water. Water poured off the hills into the river Till which runs south towards Stapleford, in Wiltshire; even the normally dry upper reaches were full and fast flowing. The river rose higher and higher and in the afternoon burst its banks at Shrewton, causing a number of houses to collapse. By late evening water was over 2 metres above normal winter level and the inhabitants of villages in the valley were full of apprehension about what the night would bring. Some were too frightened to remain in their homes and went to stay with friends; others who remained took their prized possessions and smaller animals upstairs and spent the rest of the night wondering what safety their houses afforded.

There was a tax on bricks at that time and as an economy measure many of the houses were built of rammed chalk, rubble and clay which was not nearly strong enough to withstand the scouring flood. Houses collapsed one by one—seventy-two in the Till valley. Three people were drowned, 200 made homeless and many deprived of most of their possessions. A disaster fund of £4000 was raised and new cottages built to better specifications at what now seems the mouth-watering cost of £40 each. The houses, with their commemorative plaque, are still standing to demonstrate the wisdom of building substantially.

Snow thaw floods   March 1947

The greater the quantity of snow lying, the larger the area affected and the quicker the thaw, the more serious are the consequences likely to be. After the particularly snowy winter at the beginning of 1947, it was not difficult to anticipate trouble during the ensuing thaw.

The war was over, but as housewives juggled their ration books between tinned fruit and jam, and invented recipes for stretching minute quantities of meat into satisfying meals, it hardly seemed a victorious peace. To cap everything, the weather turned cold after a very wet first half of January, and a month of easterly winds brought prolonged periods of air frost till the beginning of March. Snow fell frequently and most of the country was snow covered between 27 January and 13 March. Fuel was in short supply; candles in use during electricity cuts and queues formed at the Gas Companies for the pleasure of wheeling home a sack of coke in an old pram. Traffic conditions were chaotic, the armed forces devoted their attention to getting supplies to isolated farms and villages, about 4 million sheep and lambs and 30,000 cattle died and thousands of tons of potatoes had been ruined in their clamps by deep frost. The winter was as disastrous as that of 1962-3, but with one important difference—more snow had accumulated and was waiting for the inevitable thaw to convert it to a mobile liquid.

It is more difficult to measure snowfall than rainfall because snow blows across level ground in any appreciable wind, and packs into drifts against obstructions; therefore depths of snow do not necessarily give an accurate measure of the quantity which has fallen. But under satisfactory measuring conditions on level ground, 600mm of freshly fallen and uncompacted snow is the equivalent of the rare 50mm falls of rain which are likely to lead to severe floods.

In 1947, snow fell somewhere or other in Britain every day between 22 January and 17 March; there were more daily falls of 600mm than occurred in 1963 and the snow drifts were every bit as deep, over 5 metres in many places. By the end of February the level depth of compacted snow on high ground in Denbigh and Teesdale was 2 metres. It all amounted to millions and millions of tons of potential thaw water.

By the evening of 10 March warm air between 7°-10°C nudged its way into the extreme south-west of England, bringing with it rain. Snow will melt at about 65mm a day in warm air alone, at about 175mm a day in warm air and sunshine, and at about 250mm a day in warm air and rain. So the scene was set for a rapid rate of thaw and the ice-hard ground beneath the snow was useless in disposing of the water. By the evening of 11 March vast areas from Somerset to Kent were turned into huge lakes. The river Avon overflowed at Salisbury and was threatening Bath; all the usual flood spots along the Thames were under water; the Medway was rising, parts of Tonbridge had 1-2 metres of water, and the Lea overflowed into Hackney marshes. In the next few days the warm air spread slowly north and east across the country. The Welsh mountains unloaded melted snow into the valleys of the Severn and the Wye, Herefordshire became almost isolated and all the Midland rivers were in full spate. Everywhere the news was the same: boats instead of cars using the roads; people rescued from top floors; communal feeding centres and evacuation from homes — all heavy blows after a hard winter and an even harder war.

In the eastern counties of England the situation was being watched anxiously. They have wide almost level plains, full of rivers which run with only the gentlest gradients towards the sea. In early centuries these rivers overflowed their banks every wet season, making a stable agriculture impossible until a Dutchman, Cornelius Vermuyden, came to England in the seventeenth century and remodelled the countryside. He worked first in south Yorkshire and then devoted the rest of his life to reclaiming and defending land in East Anglia. He built embankments along the rivers, a little distance from the natural banks, to provide washland in time of flood and grazing land at other times. He built two short cuts between Earith and Denver on the Great Ouse to help cope with the water from all the tributaries. He protected the land behind a criss-cross of dykes and gradually the fertile land gained an important status as supplier of staple foods for the nation's larder. The climate helps by being on average sunnier and drier than many other parts of the country.

Ever since the defences were built it had been appreciated that their success depended upon good maintenance. What had not been anticipated was the extreme shrinkage of the peat subsoil under the reclaimed land. As marshland dried out the peat shrank, the topsoil level fell — 3 metres in 84 years at Holme Fen near Peterborough. The process is continuing and, since the river beds have to be kept at their proper level in order to maintain the flow of water to the sea, the floodwalls have had to be continually reinforced. Rain water surplus to requirements in the lower lying fields has to be pumped from the lower drains up into the rivers which are now sometimes above roof level of sur-

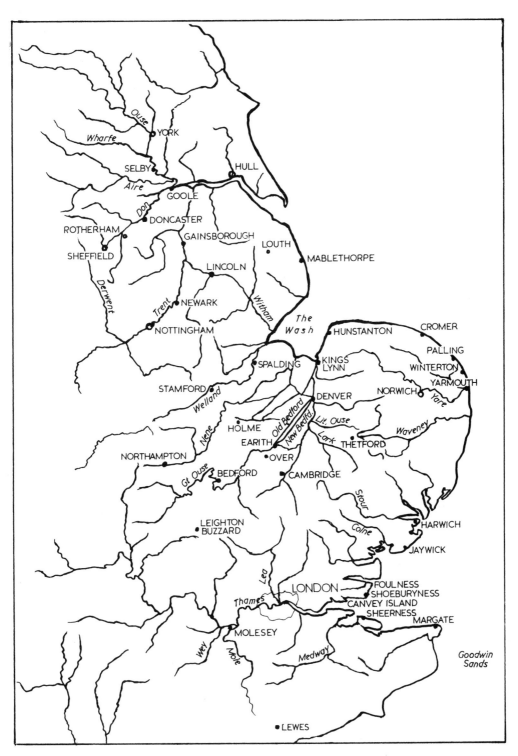

Eastern England, below sea level in many places and under constant threat from the North Sea.

rounding buildings. Despite the flatness of the terrain, therefore, there is the same potential danger of water falling from a height as there is in hilly country.

By Thursday, 13 March 1947, several Norfolk rivers were at, or just below, safety level and the Cottenham Lode was overspilling. The Catchment Boards which administer the Fens waterways have special procedures for flood emergencies—farmers are enrolled in gangs, sacks of clay stored at strategic positions, or loaded on barges or in lorries, hurricane lamps and torches are at the ready. From Friday, the 14th, the scheme was put into operation and the banks patrolled day and night from then on. Water was overspilling in several places on Saturday, but a judicious use of sandbags, tarpaulins and clay staved off breaches in the dykes in about a dozen places.

Perhaps the weather thought that man was resisting its authority too successfully and set out to prove who was master. A depression in the Atlantic advanced and deepened, bringing rain and severe SW gales and

by Sunday afternoon wind had increased in southern England to about 65mph, gusting nearer 100mph. It whipped up waves on all flood waters, stripped many roofs and, in London, destroyed two houses. In the eastern counties, wind could hardly have blown in a worse direction—along the line of the major rivers—and it was piling up the water before it into waves which were dashing the banks of many washlands. The country is as flat as the proverbial pancake in the Fen country and there are few hedges or clumps of trees to break the force of the wind. Sometimes the only windbreaks are the dykes themselves, but the men working on repairs had to be on *top* of these banks, not sheltering to leeward.

Sunday night was horrific. Communications between the gangs of men and their headquarters at Ely were almost non-existent. Telegraph poles had blown down, roads were impassable because of water or uprooted trees, the electricity supply at Ely had failed and the outpost gangs could not keep their hurricane lamps alight. At times the wind tore away the emergency clay-bag repairs and the

The particularly snowy winter of 1947 resulted in extensive thaw floods afterwards during March. Much agricultural land in eastern counties is below river level and was inundated when the dykes were breached in various places. Pictured here is the breach at Over on 20 March 1947. *(Daily Mirror)*

men could hardly stand against the buffeting wind. Sheer determination averted many disasters, particularly on the river Lark near Prickwillow and West Roe, but determination was not always enough.

About 6pm two gangs of men who had been working all day on the banks of the Great Ouse near Over discovered a crack in the dyke. The light was failing, they struggled to repair the damage but it was like children trying to save a sandcastle against the incoming tide—useless. By 9pm the men had no strength left. Water was pouring round one end of the emergency wall of bags, nearby villages had been warned and farmers were hastily preparing to evacuate. The workmen gave up the struggle and two hours later the Great Ouse broke its banks with a tremendous rush, spread unimpeded into Willington Fen submerging everything in its way till it reached the southern bank of the Old West River. Troops were drafted in on Monday morning to help, but nothing could prevent these dyke walls being eroded from the rear; the floods poured across the old West River and then across the other side into Haddenham Fen.

The Little Ouse was also breached in two places and flooded towards Lakenheath and Hockwold. The Ely Ouse burst at Little Thetford inundating 2000 acres of farmland in the Thetford and Stretham Fens. The River Wissey broke its banks into Hilgay North Fen and later into Feltwell. The River Welland flooded Spalding and caused much damage with ice floes—a particularly ironical happening since a scheme for improving local waterways had been approved but postponed because of the exigencies of war. East Anglia was a grim picture of swirling water bearing household goods, agricultural equipment and dead livestock, and all this was mirrored by conditions further north.

The River Trent flooded in many places and trouble eventually spread to Nottingham itself; the town had expanded unwisely in the nineteenth century by building the suburb of West Bridgford into the natural floodland of the river. In the early hours of 18 March the river claimed back what it considered its own, and hundreds of homes were flooded, often up to first-floor level. By the time the swollen river reached the tidal reaches of the Humber and met spring tides from the sea, the whole lower Trent valley was flooded, Gainsborough being awash to the eaves of some cottages and Norton suffering a burst in the sharp bend of the river banks.

West of London the rivers all continued to rise after the dreadful Sunday gale and by Thursday, the 20th, four times as much water was pouring over Teddington weir into the tidal reaches of the Thames as was flowing on 11 March. London itself suffered little from the Thames on that occasion, except for choking of filters at Lots Power Station which temporarily put the London Underground out of action. But the rivers Roding and Lea flooded many homes in north London and damaged filter beds at Lea Bridge water works, so that whilst everyone there was sick to death of water, water everywhere, there was not a drop to drink except that brought in by water cart! After 20 March floods in the West Country subsided, but eastern counties still faced a life and death struggle.

The Don spilled over into Rotherham and Doncaster, while the village of Bentley was swamped and its coal mine only just saved. The Wharfe, the Yorkshire Ouse, the Derwent and the Aire all burst their banks and flooded into huge areas between York and

It required great ingenuity to repair some of the dyke breaches. Royal Engineers, assisted by prisoners of war, used Neptune tanks to fill the gap in the river Ouse at Over prior to making the permanent repair. *(Daily Mirror)*

Goole, which included some of the largest food processing plants in the country. By an unkind turn of fate there were specially high tides up the Humber during the week commencing 23 March and gallons of salt and fresh water mixture were liberally laced with dissolved sugar and edible oils. Selby, the town at the cross roads of all these floods, was practically drowned — 70 per cent of all the houses were under water — , only the Old Abbey and a few streets round the market place remained dry. The population was fed by field kitchens in the market square, iron rations came into the town from elsewhere and after dark life carried on by candlelight.

The floods in the Fens were still rising on 24 March when the Government pledged full support for the area and attention could be diverted a little from the task of rescue to the long business of repair. Major breaches, such as the 50 metre gap in the Great Ouse near Over, taxed ingenuity to the extreme; there, the Royal Engineers assisted by prisoners of war used amphibious tanks to form a box round the breach while a secure wall of clay was built outside. At Crowland, amphibious tanks were lined up to form a temporary wall, and near Southery mattresses of brush wood and willow were sunk into the gap in the Wissery and hastily piled high with clay. Not all the breaches were mended at the first attempt because there were renewed gales and rain at the beginning of April to give further setbacks.

Meanwhile an armada of pumps was converging on the area, loaned by the armed forces, local authorities and private firms both in Britain and in Holland, which had always been well versed in the clearance problems of low lying ground. Engineers surveyed the floods by air to determine where the pumps could best be used, but getting them into position was a colossal problem in itself, because often the greatest need was in the most inaccessible places. A hundred volunteer firemen came to help work the pumps, petrol rationing formalities were waived and the great suck started.

Shallow water was quickly cleared but it was well into May, in some places June, before all the land re-emerged. Farmers returned to their homes to repair damage, clear ditches, renew livestock and purchase new feeding stuffs. An unholy stench of rotting potatoes and decaying animal corpses lay over the area. The prospect for any sort of crops that year seemed remote; however, farmers were encouraged to do what they could by a promise from the government to bear part of the financial risk. So they ploughed round the edge of fields as the water receded and within weeks crops were sprouting—Haddenham Fen alone being unable to reclaim in time for any planting. The rest of the summer was good and a reasonable harvest was brought in.

These floods were of *fresh* water, however. Recovery from *salt* water would have taken very much longer.

9

Have I not heard the sea puffed up with winds rage like an angry boar

William Shakespeare

It is no good pretending any longer that the sea is always the ultimate safe depository for all flood water, because it isn't. Sometimes chance combinations of wind and tide pile the sea itself into such close confines that it breaks over the coast line and floods the very land it is supposed to be draining.

Tides occur because of the gravitational pull on the sea by the sun and moon, with other heavenly bodies exerting their mite of influence as well. At times of full and new moon, when the forces act in a straight line, they produce specially high and low tides, called 'spring' tides. When the sun and moon pull at angles to each other, the difference between high and low tides is much less, the least occurring at 'neap tides'. The details are complicated because the relative positions of sun and moon do not repeat themselves exactly each month, and because there is nearly two days' lag before the full effect of the position of the moon is felt.

In the Atlantic the tide resembles a wave undulation of about 1 metre in height, but when the sea divides to flow round the British Isles—up the west coast of Ireland, up the Irish Sea and along the English Channel—tides become very complex. Wherever the

sea squeezes through constricting straits the tide amplitude increases, and whenever the sea encounters further island obstructions it divides again round either side. Since the tide takes time to travel round the whole complicated coastline, time of arrival and height varies at every place. Fortunately, all these factors are predictable and are combined together into a yearly timetable which is the nautical bible for all those who work or take their recreation on the sea.

However, official tide predictions are subject to errors caused by more unpredictable weather factors, particularly atmospheric pressure. This acts as a sort of plunger on the sea surface, depressing the level when pressure is high and allowing it to rise if pressure is low. When the weather situation is stationary or only changing slowly, the difference in level is hardly noticeable and only amounts to a matter of about 120mm in the level of the sea for a pressure difference of 10 mbs. But, when pressure changes rapidly with the advance and departure of a vigorous depression, the plunger effect is rapid enough to start wave surges with peaks and troughs of much greater amplitude. When unhappy chance causes both surge and gale winds to drive the sea into a tight corner at high tide, disastrous consequences can result.

The Bristol Channel is one vulnerable area when the wind is from the west or south-west, and it was undoubtedly the surge effect of the passing depression in the Great Storm of 1703 (p33) which made flooding so bad in the Severn Valley. On the other side of the country, the Thames estuary has the disadvantage of being also in the constricting southern basin of the North Sea. When the tide down the east coast of Scotland and England gets chased by strong northerly winds behind a vigorous depression moving south down the North Sea, the surge effect can tip the balance from safe high water to disastrous floods. The narrow Straits of Dover are quite inadequate as a 'plughole' for accommodating the press of water, which then takes the easiest route available, up the Thames estuary.

London flood   6 January 1928

London's first defence against the Thames has always been walls, some of which date back to Roman times. Henry VI appointed special commissioners to see that walls were properly maintained and kept to a specified height, and the Metropolitan Water Board took over these duties in 1897. The prescribed height of the walls was raised in 1881 and remained the same until 1928.

It had been a white Christmas over southern England in 1927; by the end of the year there was about 300mm of snow lying on level ground with huge drifts in open country. Snow started to melt on 31 December and the thaw was general by 2 January 1928. Then a deep depression passed north of the British Isles and heavy rain combined with thaw water to give widespread flooding along the Thames and its tributaries.

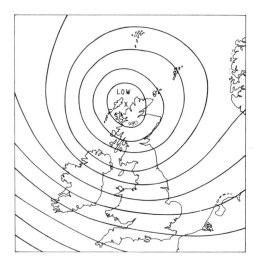

0600 GMT 6 January 1928. A deep depression from the Atlantic was centred over Scotland and then decided to change course towards the south-east.

In the early hours of 6 January a small depression just west of the Hebrides deepened rapidly and started to move south-east and then down the North Sea. During the day strong WSW winds piled up water in the English Channel towards the Straits of Dover, but as the depression moved towards Denmark pressure over the North Sea rose as fast as it had fallen, and wind veered to between north and north-west, still at gale strength. A spring tide was expected and the already overfull Thames was flowing fast against the sea trying to come up-river.

High water at Southend that night was 1.5 metres above predicted level and 17 minutes early in arriving. By the time the flood tide reached central London it was 1.8m above predicted level, which was 0.3m higher than any previous record. By midnight the wind had fallen to light but the indelible effect of the day's events was approaching a climax in London. Flood reports started coming in from Battersea, Poplar and Greenwich; the embank-

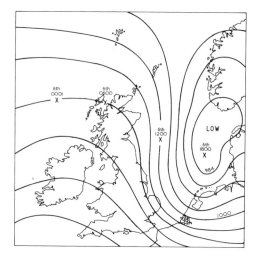

1800 GMT 6 January 1928. The rapid movement towards Denmark, giving fast-falling pressure ahead of the depression and fast-rising pressure behind, caused a surge of water up the Thames estuary. Much flooding and damage resulted.

ment at Temple Station was awash and the whole of Old Palace Yard, Westminster, was above the ankles in water. Waves washed the walls of Temple Gardens and the training ship *President* towered over the scene at embankment parapet level.

The embankment in front of the Tate Gallery was the first to give way under the strain and the Gallery was flooded almost to the tops of doors on the ground floor. A valuable collection of Turner pictures was submerged but managed to survive the rough and ready treatment of being taken out of their frames and spread like botanical specimens to dry. Some Landseer pictures were ruined by the ordeal of water.

Lots Power Station was partly flooded and so was Wandsworth Gas Works and the Blackwall tunnel.

Flood water found it child's-play to lift paving blocks in Grosvenor Road, London, on 6 January 1928, when the Thames surge drowned fourteen people in basements. *(Daily Mirror)*

Barking Creek river wall gave way and the sewage works were flooded, and the Tower of London once again found itself with water in normally dry moats. Near Lambeth Bridge the culminating tragedy was played out when 25 metres of embankment broke under the pressure of water and flooded basements of houses with such rapidity that many people could not escape. By the time one man woke to awareness of the water swilling around his bedroom, he was unable to open the door to his children's room because of the water inside. His four children were drowned while he remained helpless outside the door. Ten other people were drowned in similar manner and the death toll would have been even greater but for the swift action of firemen and mounted police knocking peremptorily on as many doors as they

could. Over 4000 people were left homeless or in distress.

The flood shocked everyone, particularly when they realised that the weather situation could have been even worse. Wind was gusting to about 60mph but many gales are stronger; the Thames was flowing fast but the rate of flow over Teddington weir, the last before the tidal reaches, was not the highest known (only about three-quarters of the rate on 20 March 1947); and though there was a spring tide that day it was not the highest predicted for the year. That expected on 25 March 1928 was nearly a metre higher. One additional peculiarity increased the realisation of possible worse disaster in the future if all extreme factors coincided. Britain is tilting along an axis across northern England, so that the north-west of

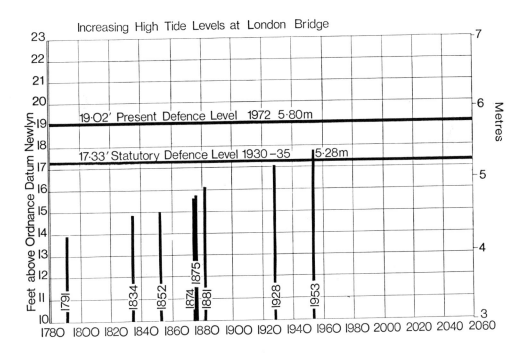

Chart showing the increasing high tide levels at London Bridge. *(Department of Public Health Engineering)*

Scotland has been rising at 0.3 metres per century while south-east England has been sinking at the same rate. This means that the effective tide height in London has been steadily rising and may continue to do so — an uncomfortable thought for a population which has been encroaching on the river's flood plains by building.

The inadequacy of the river walls was discussed at length in 1928 and their height was raised a little. However, this is not an operation which can be carried out indefinitely because it must be done along the whole length to be effective and this gets more difficult each time. It is not just a matter of adding a few more courses of brick but of reconstructing to meet new pressures. This involves alteration to wharves and approach roads and perhaps demolition of property, after which the people made safe behind high walls have probably lost the amenity value of the river altogether.

A programme of research was started by the Meteorological Office and the Liverpool Observatory and Tidal Institute to study storm surges and the deviation of observed tide height from those predicted. A flood warning system for the capital was inaugurated, based on an agreed danger level at Southend where high water is $1\frac{1}{2}$ hours earlier than at London Bridge. And talk again returned to the idea of a barrage across the Thames.

Such a project had been discussed after a similar storm on 29 November 1897 had caused flooding in the Thames estuary. The suggested site was between Tilbury and Gravesend; the barrage would have contained locks and sluices and would have carried roads and tunnels for traffic. The estimated cost in 1907 was £5 million, to be defrayed by revenue from the Port of London and by tolls on traffic. Nothing came of the idea, then or in 1927. There were criticisms about handicaps to shipping, difficulty of drainage, possible raising of the water table below buildings on the upper side of the barrage, silting up — all understandable procrastinations when faced with a vast scheme whose side effects could not be proved conclusively.

But in 1953 there occurred what may well become known as the worst weather disaster of the century. London itself suffered little but the experiences of its close neighbours left no mistake about the writing on the wall. One day a critical combination of high tide, weather and sinking land level could devastate the capital if nothing were done. A 60,000-word report was compiled by a team of experts and started its slow way through the 'usual channels'. In 1974 the principle was accepted that a Thames Barrier should be built for completion by 1978 and preliminary work has been started on the chosen Woolwich site. May it be finished before the crisis comes.

Meanwhile, let me tell you about the storm which jolted the complacency of London in 1953.

Scotland   31 January 1953
On Thursday, 29 January 1953, a depression detached itself from a stationary low pressure system north of the Azores and started moving first NE and then ENE. It deepened rapidly from about 1003 mbs to 979 mbs by Friday evening, when it was about 105 miles north of Scotland and still deepening at about 1 mb per hour. By breakfast on Saturday the 31st, it had reached its lowest value of 968 mbs and was centred just east of Scotland, having decided to alter course towards the south-east.

Further out in mid-Atlantic an anticyclone was intensifying and thus

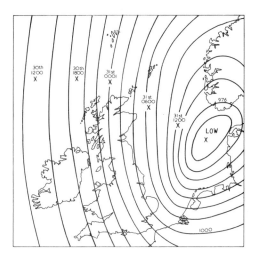

1800 GMT 31 January 1953. The worst storm Britain has suffered in the twentieth century. The isobaric situation was almost identical to that of 6 January 1928 except that pressure behind the depression rose rapidly over a much larger area, and the North Sea surge was much greater.

tightening the pressure gradient behind the depression. Gale warnings from the Met Office were justified with a vengeance and by noon northerly winds were screeching down the western side of the British Isles. For an hour the anemometer on the Orkney Islands showed a mean speed of 90mph with gusts up to 125mph. The isobars on the midday weather chart were closely packed together to indicate a wind of 175mph over an area 100 miles wide. These speeds were higher than anything previously recorded and had fatal consequences for the forests of Scotland. More trees were blown down than are normally felled in a year and some owners lost all their timber. It was on a par with the damage to woodland in the south of England by the 1703 hurricane.

It was far from comfortable at sea, which claimed the *Clan Macquarrie,* a cargo vessel bound from Hull to the Clyde, as its first victim. The ship had passed Cape Wrath in north Scotland during the night while the depression was to the west and SW gales were blowing. She had intended to head down the Minch, between Lewis and the mainland, but then decided to take the longer route outside Lewis in order to gain more sea room. Before she could achieve enough for safety, the depression had passed away south-eastwards and the wind had veered to NW. She was driven on to the western shore of Lewis in the early hours of 31 January and pounded against the rocks. Her fuel tanks burst and made the rocks slimy; snow showers were falling in the bitterly cold airstream and in this always exposed place rescuers had a formidable task to manhandle rockets and breeches buoy equipment across fields and into position in the tortuous icy conditions. They managed to get a line aboard the *Clan Macquarrie* by daylight and sixty-six men were brought ashore by breeches buoy in continuing bad weather.

All around the shores of Britain vessels were in trouble and found shelter where and if they could. Normal shipping movement ceased and Lloyds register later recorded 8 vessels missing and over 300 lives lost in home waters — 133 of them from one vessel, the ferry boat *Princess Victoria.*

The *Princess Victoria* plied daily from Stranraer, on the west coast of Scotland, to Larne in Ireland. Stranraer is tucked deep into the neck of Loch Ryan, about 10 miles from the narrow exit to the sea, and the strength of the wind outside the shelter of the loch was not fully appreciated when Captain Ferguson prepared to sail at 7.45am. on Saturday, 31 January. The ferry crossings were part of the regular pattern of life in that area and took place whatever the weather. By the time the ferry was half-way up the loch

101

it experienced enough swell to indicate the conditions outside. Life-lines were rigged on the open deck and everything was secured for a rough passage in the normal routine of good seamanship.

The open sea was very confused because of the alternation of gale wind directions in the past 24 hours and it seems likely that the Captain decided that he did not like the look of things and tried to return to Stranraer. In starting to turn he must have taken a huge wave on the stern which forced ajar the steel doors to the car deck. Water was half a metre deep when the damage was discovered, and the doors were too buckled to be closed.

From then on the captain had little freedom of action. He dare not continue back to Stranraer because, with the sea on his stern, the incoming water would cause the ship to founder. He probably disliked going further into the wind because he could have met even bigger seas and been further from help. So he turned eastward towards Ireland, as the lesser of several evils, having just enough power to make slow progress.

Sea water was meanwhile doing its deadly work in the car deck, swishing around from side to side and eventually dislodging some vehicles from their fastenings. The ship developed a list to starboard which gradually got worse as she limped towards Ireland.

On shore the coastguard station at Portpatrick was on the alert. The first message from the *Princess Victoria* came about 9.45am and said she was hove-to not under command and urgently in need of a tug; but the message was not preceded by the letters SOS denoting immediate danger. The SOS came three-quarters of an hour later, giving her position as 4 miles NW of Corsewall point and stated that she had a heavy list, was not

under command and required immediate assistance. The wind and the sea had caused the ship's damage, but the seed of the ensuing disaster lay in misunderstandings about these ship-to-shore messages.

At no time had the *Princess Victoria* mentioned that she was still heading under engine power for the Irish coast. The coastguards understood the phrase 'not under command' to mean that she had *no* power. They had estimated the position of the ship according to drift by sea and wind alone, and when the *Princess Victoria* stated she had a list of 35° which was too great to allow use of her radar, the coastguards disbelieved her estimated position in favour of their own. A destroyer and a lifeboat were soon searching the area designated by the coastguards but they had no success because the ship was much further west. Because of the pounding seas and a driving snow storm, visibility was negligible so that neither rescue boats nor searching aircraft could see the distressed vessel. The radio signals received at Portpatrick from the *Princess Victoria* gave a bearing only; the bearings received at other stations and which could have given an accurate fix on the distressed vessel were treated with caution because they were received over mountainous country and therefore subject to distortion. Ironically, they were correct.

Soon after 1pm the *Princess Victoria* reported herself on her beam ends and her engines stopped because of water, the first intimation to the searchers of the dreadful misunderstanding about her power. A quarter of an hour later she said she was about to abandon ship, and then she reported sighting the Irish Coast. The rescue vessels altered course at once, three ships in Belfast Lough left their shelter to give assistance but by this time the *Princess*

Victoria had turned over with the weight of water aboard. Launching the lifeboats had been delayed in the hope of rescue boats arriving in time because the seas were immense. When at last they attempted it, the task was impossible. One lifeboat was lowered and broke adrift with only one man aboard, quite insufficient for control. Three other boats were cut free and managed to float away as the ship went down. One boat had 29 persons in it, another had only 6 people and no oars, and the last was filled with women and children. This latter boat was almost clear of the sinking ferry when a wave lifted it high and dashed it against the stern to throw everyone into the sea. A few reached the litter of life rafts strewing the water, the remainder had no chance at all. The first ship to arrive at the scene, the *Orcy*, was helpless to reach the people struggling in the water. She had a very high bulwark rail, she would have been a menance to those in the sea if her propellers were kept turning, yet she dared not turn them off because then she would have drifted down on people to leeward. By the time suitable rescue vessels arrived many people had drowned, being too weak to cling to the rafts any longer. Out of the crew of 49 and 125 passengers, only 41 were saved, and the captain went down with his ship.

East Coast surge floods   1 February 1953

The dreadful news about the *Princess Victoria* was in everyone's minds that evening of 31 January. All down the east coast of England the weather was wild, but it did not occur to people that any calamity was in the offing. They had been out at their usual Saturday entertainments but were having a hard struggle to battle against the wind on their way home. Gale warnings were repeated on the BBC and there was mention of heavy seas pounding the Yorkshire coast but somehow that merely seemed to promise dramatic pictures in the newspapers next day. The Met Office had warned at midday about conditions favourable for abnormally high tides in the Thames during the next 24 hours, and police and river boards had been circularised with the information as usual. They had had sixty similar warnings in the past eight years and no one was particularly worried though a few observant seamen were uneasy about the poor ebb of the afternoon tide. By 10pm the sea was overtopping sea walls in Northumberland, Durham and Yorkshire and pouring inland wherever the coast was fully exposed to the NW wind. The Wash was an open invitation to the sea and the north coast of Norfolk was taking a wicked pounding. But at that time there was no mechanism for relaying all this information in quantitative terms to all the other places further down the coast, and the sea was piling inexorably onwards round the coast of Suffolk to the Essex and Kent jaws of the Thames estuary.

The Essex coast is low lying and much of it has been reclaimed from the sea. Over the centuries rivers have carried down silt to the sea which threw it back again in tides, impregnated with seeds of salt-loving plants. These took root and bound the silt into areas called saltings which eventually built up enough so that only the highest tides covered them. Rain washed the salt out of the soil, shallow fresh-water plants were able to exist and the saltings became good pasture —so good that, wherever there was danger that the sea would bite back into it again, protective walls were built. Islands of reclaimed land hug the Essex coast, looking like fortresses from outside and like shallow saucers inside, for the land shrank in the drying out process behind its safe defences and is now often below the height of spring tides.

Maintenance of these walls has always been a problem. Originally they were the responsibility of private owners who often lacked money, labour and any co-ordinating scheme. Latterly, under the authority of public bodies, more unified defences of a much higher engineering standard have been possible, but the persistently increasing height of tides has conspired to make them still inadequate. Recent history emphasises this fact with a trail of sea floods. On 29 November 1897, one-third of Foulness Island was flooded and its walls were then raised by a small amount. In January 1928, when London flooded, Bridgmarsh Island in the River Crouch was inundated and Canvey Isle escaped by a hair's breadth. On 12-13 February 1938 a North Sea surge burst over the Norfolk coast to flood 15 square miles around Horsey, and the Essex walls suffered enough to alert the experts that still all was not well. On 1 March 1949 the sea again lapped frighteningly at Canvey Isle. In 1953 the sea carried out its threats.

By 11pm on 31 January Essex police and river authorities were patrolling their boundaries with the southern North Sea basin. The northerly wind was off-shore here but this was doing little to hold back the prodigious waves. The sea was splashing over the walls everywhere; streets, gardens and houses behind were running with water but the main sea walls were all holding well. So the sea chose to demonstrate its power with a series of rearguard actions. About midnight, part of the sea wall inside the mouth of the river Stour and just beyond the harbour of Harwich collapsed and the sea poured

into the old marsh basin called Bathside. One man, walking along the road, saw a wall of water advancing towards him and only just managed to reach his house and shut the door behind him before the water arrived. In less than a minute the water had broken down his front door and he was screaming to his wife to get the children up. By the time he managed to carry them in turn to slightly higher ground, water was up to his chest, and for the final rescue of his dog he had to swim both ways. In 15 minutes the whole Bathside area and some dozen streets of houses were under water, and the sea continued to pour in through the gap till it overflowed the railway embankment and into the rest of Harwich. Most of the houses here were two-storey and people could retreat upstairs.

Further down the coast is Jaywick Sands, a holiday resort noted for its fine sandy beaches. Concrete walls along the front defended some avenues of bungalows and summer chalets

Jaywick Sands and its wooden bungalows were flooded in August 1948 when the protective sea walls were breached. No lives were lost on that occasion though holidaymakers lost some of their possessions. On 1 February 1953 the invasion by the sea was so violent that sometimes people could only escape by punching a hole in the flimsy ceilings and climbing into tiny lofts. (Daily Mirror)

leading back from the shore. Behind these homes was an old clay wall, then another area of chalets and caravans sandwiched between it and yet another wall. The mere existence of three lines of defence underlined the impertinence of putting buildings there at all and the sea was about to make the point as forcibly as it could. While the patrols were watching the front and assessing the overtopping sea water as not unduly serious, the sea burst through walls around the Colne estuary to the west. What appeared to an observer to be a tidal wave advanced swiftly across St Osyth Marsh towards Jaywick, tearing up the grass and any other debris in its way. It burst through the *rear* counter walls of Jaywick and filled the Grassland and Brooklands areas to a depth of 3 metres in a few minutes. The doors of the flimsy homes burst open and the rooms became hideous maelstroms of water and crashing furniture. Those who slept soundly or reacted slowly to the noise which awoke them were drowned in their beds. Other people managed to climb on to tables, then to clutch the tops of doors, fanlights, anything still rigid, as the tables floated away from under them. Some had time to knock a hole in the ceiling with a chair, haul themselves and their families up into the tiny rafter space, there to remain in sodden night clothes for the rest of the night, shivering, shocked, and aghast at the drowned home below. Others who had not had the thought or the strength to do this remained standing as high as they could, clutching children, husbands or wives till one or other died of exposure in the icy water or, exhausted, slipped under to drown. Those watching from the outside higher sea walls were helpless to do anything much. There were no boats to immediate hand and even if there had been the current was too

strong to make progress. The most they could do was wade into some shallower depths to answer the cries of distress and to lead a few people out to safety to the occasional oases of higher ground.

Meanwhile the islands off the Crouch estuary were receiving contemptuous treatment from the sea, being all overtopped and flooded. Foulness suffered breaches in a mile of sea wall facing the mouth of the Crouch and the island once more became a sea. The 300 inhabitants were marooned in their farmhouses, woken out of sleep by the cries of farm animals being submerged in their pens and stables. They recognised the extent of water by the silvery moonlit ripples all around and in the morning they measured its height by the tree tops just visible above the surface. Birds, hares and rabbits crowded every exposed branch and every knoll of dry ground was packed tight with cattle and sheep.

At Great Wakering, just inland from Shoeburyness, thirty-seven families on a nissen hut estate awoke to find water lapping their beds. Some acted quickly and staggered through the rising water to the higher main road near by, but the current was fast and many were afraid to take the icy plunge. They remained till they saw they might become engulfed and then climbed out of windows to cling in the howling wind to the rounded roofs. Gymnastics such as these were for the young only and one middle-aged couple spent the whole night standing on their heavy stoves with water up to their chests.

Then it was the turn of Canvey Isle, 250 acres of holiday resort separated by a moat of creeks from the mainland and with only one connecting link, Benfleet Bridge. The sea mounted a flank attack once again, piling into

Hadleigh Ray, constricting further into Small Gains Creek and Tewkes Creek till the protective walls found the strain too great. Cracks started to let water through and were seen by a patrolling waterboard man who appreciated the ominous threat and raced down the road knocking on people's doors. Because of this, some families had already got to safety in their lofts via outside staircases when the Small Gains Creek wall suddenly breached. The sea poured in and carried with it sheds, bicycles, bushes, anything in its path. Many bungalow doors were burst open, to cause the same havoc inside as at Jaywick. Some people, whose doors held, deliberately opened the way for the sea because they felt their own safety depended on getting to their outside staircases and into the lofts. They clung to cupboards to withstand the first rush of water and then clutched at every gutter, post or window-sill to haul themselves against the current to their staircases. People acted instinctively to the requirements of the moment and later wondered where they found the strength to do what they did. The elderly man who broke his neighbour's window in order to get her out and on to his shoulder and back to his own house higher up could never have done so if he had had time to think. The woman who swam to her outside staircase against the current, made a rope from bedding in the loft and hauled first her baby and then her two older children up from the lower window, and finally helped her husband over the upper sill, was drawing upon some quite unsuspected store of strength. While the child who complied with the hideous order to climb out of a window and up the face of a house, still dazed with sleep and only supported by a rope of sheets, must have found some quite unexpec-

ted trust in his parents.

Further down the estuary, industry was taking a similar pounding. The petroleum empires at Coryton, Shell-haven and Thames Haven were swamped and only very prompt action in closing down the distillation units prevented petrol escaping to make a bad situation worse. At Purfleet, flood water tumbled sacks of sugar and reels of newspaper out of warehouses and laced them liberally with the contents of a margarine factory. Oil drums clattered against the metal sheds of railway sidings and a dozen oil tankers were lifted off their railway lines to subside later in a neat ring-a-roses circle astride another line. Tilbury was extensively flooded, but stealthily from the marshland behind with sufficient time for householders to establish themselves safely upstairs. There was patchy flooding right to the centre of London where the tide was abnormally high but safely contained behind embankment walls. The saving grace for the capital was that the river flow down the Thames was not particularly great and so the greedy sea could be accommodated.

The newspapers propped up on Sunday breakfast tables next morning contained remarkably little detail about the night's events down the east coast. Communications had been disrupted everywhere and not even the people on the spot were sure what was happening around them. Lights had failed, the moon later disappeared, fire engines and ambulances were halted by water from the very areas they were needed most, and no boats were conveniently at hand in the middle of the winter night. But though there was no central direction of rescue in the first confusion, the usual pattern of British floods spontaneously evolved. Common sense and desperate urgency created small rescue

106

nuclei wherever there was dry ground, sometimes a café, sometimes a school, sometimes a private home. British and American servicemen left their remote stations to join rescuers in the crisis areas, wading waist deep through water to support terrified people back to the dry havens where they were given hot drinks, wrapped in blankets, coats, jerseys, or anything dry to replace their sodden nightclothes. Everyone with a smattering of nursing knowledge was acting doctor to the best of their ability, binding gashes, treating for shock and exposure, even for frostbite, and coping till professional help became available. Officials of voluntary and civic organisations who were called out of bed knew they had an emergency of unknown proportions to deal with but the immensity of the problem was not revealed till daylight.

Northumberland, Durham and Yorkshire all had flooded areas, most of the Lincolnshire coast north of the Wash was under water, Mablethorpe and Sutton having been evacuated as far as the darkness of the night permitted. In Norfolk 1½ miles of bungalows along the sea front at Hunstanton had been almost entirely washed away and twelve US servicemen drowned in attempting rescues. The sea stretched miles inland of Kings Lynn and the Great Ouse had broken its banks in several places. At Snettisham bungalows had been dashed against the flood wall and left like matchwood. Cley and Salthouse had been devastated by the sea as badly as if by enemy bombing. The sea had claimed many lives and homes in Sea Palling, and the tidy concrete and tarmac promenade at Cromer was broken up as if by pneumatic drill. Parts of Yarmouth and Gorleston were flooded and the tide surging up the long narrow estuary of the River Yare had filled Breydon Water with violent waves which breached the walls and claimed back again the old marshland on the south side. The north coast of Kent also had large areas of

The problems of rescue are enormous. Here a blind man had to be helped through a bedroom window of a house flooded in Maplethorpe during the east coast floods of 1 February 1953. (Daily Mirror)

The sea showed no mercy to the Norfolk village of Sea Palling when it burst through the defensive walls on 1 February 1953. (Eastern Daily News)

The raging sea brought sand with it when it invaded Sutton on Sea, Lincs., after sweeping away the sea wall. Roads were covered in sand to a depth of over one metre and the ground floors of these houses were barricaded behind sand banks. 3 February 1953.

inundation and the 20-metre high stone lighthouse at Margate had been smashed to pieces. The submarine *Sirdar* had sunk at Sheerness and the frigate *Berkely* capsized, fortunately without loss of life.

The North Sea exacted a fierce toll: some 200,000 flooded acres; damage to property, industry and livestock beyond estimation, and a total death toll of 307, of which 58 were on Canvey Isles and 35 at Jaywick. It hardly seemed possible that anywhere else could have suffered worse from one storm, but Holland certainly did. That low-lying country was completely exposed to the main force of the wind and sea surge, and many of her dykes

Harbours gave no safety to boats on 1 February 1953 when the North Sea surge simply picked up vessels and dumped them ashore. *(Daily Mirror)*

Canvey Isle was entirely flooded apart from a few oases of dry land. Boats of all shapes and sizes arrived to help evacuate the islanders. 1 February 1953. *(Daily Mirror)*

Five days after the North Sea surge floods of 1 February 1953 a householder in Belvedere, Kent, returned to salvage what she could from her home. Three black grimy tidemarks were visible on her walls, and the rest of her home was afloat. *(Daily Mirror)*

Some of the hardest tasks were to rescue animals. Sheep often had sodden fleeces which made them too heavy to lift and as cargo in small rowing boats they made the craft dangerously unstable. 3 February 1953. *(Daily Mirror)*

Cattle marooned on dry ground surrounding a farm house after the surge floods of 1 February 1953. Few cattle relished plunging into water to get to new pastures and farmers often had to use stampeding tactics to get them to move. *(Daily Mirror)*

collapsed during a phenomenal press of water just before high tide. Nearly half a million acres of reclaimed land were swallowed again by the sea; 1800 people were drowned and over 50,000 had to be evacuated.

During Sunday, 1 February, a web of organisation imperceptibly built up in England to continue and support the prodigious efforts of individuals the previous night. Boats were commandeered and manhandled to the places most needed, even fragile dinghies and canoes having a contribution to make because grass and debris often fouled anything powered by outboard motor. Rescue was often very difficult, specially when it came to lifting bedridden people from upper windows or helping those paralysed by cold from their roof top perches. Dispersal of evacuees depended upon the numbers affected. Where the

flooded area was small and compact, like the nissen hut estate at Great Wakering, the villages coped with their own problem, getting people away gradually by boats and thence to the private homes of villagers. Even at Jaywick, with its own flood victims, a stream of voluntary drivers and ambulances spirited away half-frozen evacuees to the welcoming warmth of private homes and seaside hotels, which unhesitatingly opened their doors when they heard of the emergency.

Canvey Isle was a special problem because of the great number of inhabitants in the 6 square miles under water. The corny platitude that 'time and tide wait for no man' had taken on a new significance for the 12,000 people on the island and they had no intention of remaining to see what horror the next high tide would bring.

A spontaneous movement of people, weirdly dressed in whatever they could grab from the flood and often without shoes, started across the Benfleet Bridge as soon as conditions made it possible. The exodus was encouraged by officials who were struggling with inadequate means of communication but had managed to organise a fleet of buses and lorries waiting at rescue points. These scooped up the exhausted people as they arrived over the bridge and took them to various schools which had been hastily opened as reception centres. As one school filled, another took over and all soon became clogged with a milling throng of bedraggled humans and animals. People — grateful for hot drinks, plimsolls from the school lockers and spare clothes conjured from local homes — were worried about members of the family they had lost touch with, dazed from the shock of bereavement, anxious to to make contact with friends to whom they could escape from the horror.

The Post Office rigged up telephone lines with a speed unbelievable to those who normally wait years for an installation; endless lists of names were compiled in school notebooks by volunteers who managed to clear themselves a tiny space in which to work, and somehow everyone's immeddiate needs were supplied.

There was no place in the reality of that day for fares on the railway to London or tickets on the buses; people just piled in and were taken to their destination without question. Petrol vouchers were issued for private cars and vehicle after vehicle drove throughout the day. It was not magic that by Sunday evening 10,000 people had been dispersed to London or local towns, but sheer hard work. It was the justification of every voluntary training scheme: the Civil Defence (never pressed so hard even during the war), the Women's Royal Voluntary Service, the Red Cross, St John's Ambulance Brigade, Boy Scouts and Girl Guides and all the other organisations which contributed. It was also a tribute to one man, the Clerk of Billericay, who realised that all the multiplicity of spontaneous individual efforts might prove useless if there were no overall directing authority. He was tempted to remain on Canvey Isle to help at first hand with the countless problems, but he decided to withdraw to his own office at Billericay, where there were full telephone communications, and set up a control centre to co-ordinate rescue and evacuation operations. It was just the sort of temporary dictatorship needed and as a result the many rest centres which coped with thousands of refugees that day were left with only a handful to accommodate for the night.

Once it was certain that all the living had been rescued from the various flooded areas, there followed the sad task of getting out the dead which no one had dared spend time on at first. And then there was the problem of rounding up stray domestic animals, often crazed with fear and likely to bite or claw the hands which tried to catch them. The rescue of farm animals was often far more difficult than the rescue of people. It was possible to cajole even frightened old ladies into tippy rowing boats but no one could talk a terrified pig out of the branches of a tree or explain to a herd of cows with painful unmilked udders that it was all to their good to leave their tiny patch of dry ground and plunge neck deep into the water around them. The attempt to bait the hungry animals with foodstuffs trailing from the back of boats either failed, or succeeded too well by causing the animals to try to get into the boats.

The most successful manoeuvre was to stampede them. The men standing waist deep in water and yelling hard to get the creatures on the move discovered their task was far harder than it always appears on the television Westerns, but they achieved many fantastic rescues eventually. It was particularly difficult to get animals off the flooded islands to the mainland. Boats often proved too unstable for the task and waterlogged sheep skins made the animals too heavy to lift into boats. Fortunately it proved possible to goad even sheep, many in lamb, to swim to safety off Poton Island.

It was obvious that clearing up, repair of walls and buildings, and the restoration of industry and agriculture were tasks too great for individuals and local authorities alone. The Government immediately authorized supplies, equipment and servicemen for urgent repairs to the sea walls. Sandbags were filled and chain-ganged across impossible ground to make temporary repairs to the breaches and these proved satisfactory for a short while. There was considerable anxiety on Wednesday, 4 February, when westerly gales occurred and the sea was rough, but fortunately the tide ebbed before reaching critical levels. On the whole the modern engineered walls had withstood the storm well and it was noticeable that where breaches had occurred it was often because of erosion from the landward side.

The Government also promised immediate technical advice, and this was not the impertinence it might at first seem when proferred to people who had had ample experience of flooding six years previously. This time there was the complication of salt. Most people appreciated the corrosive nature of salt, and industry lost no time in dismantling and cleaning machinery. In general, factories got back into production much quicker than had been expected. But the urgency of cleaning agricultural machinery did not always seem a first priority to farmers who had living beasts to rescue, dead animals to burn and homes, ditches and fields to be cleared of mud and debris. They got magnificent help from local service engineers and from manufacturers who often supplied spare parts free of charge, but nevertheless the task was too great and much agricultural machinery was ruined for good.

Farmers appreciated the danger of salt water for their herds and helped each other in providing grazing and fresh water supplies. It was a matter that required constant vigilance, however, since ditches and ponds which appeared fresh at the time of testing sometimes acquired a high salt content later when flood water percolated through from adjoining fields. In some areas there was no rain for about a fortnight after flood water receded and then there was often a lag of another fortnight before the salt was washed away and grass pronounced fit to eat.

It was much more difficult for the technical advisers to restrain farmers from a natural desire to dig and plough their land as soon as the floods subsided, like they did after the 1947 thaw floods. It was not so much a matter of agriculture as of chemistry. Soil consists of particles of clay, silt and sand, and the various combinations of these give rise to agricultural soils which also contain lime, minerals, chalk and decayed vegetable matter. The two latter are good binding materials and a soil is said to have a good tilth when the smallest particles are bound together by these natural cements into larger crumbs, with adequate air spaces between so that plant roots can breathe and water can percolate slowly downwards.

When salt water invades a soil where the binding material is mainly calcium, the sodium element in the water knocks away the calcium from the soil particles leaving them bereft of their usual cohesive material. The damage is not apparent at first because the salt itself is able to do the binding job, giving the soil the appearance of a good tilthe suitable for immediate working. However, the first rains wash away the salt leaving sand and silt components to wash down slopes into ditches and drains in a wasteful slurry and leaving clay from which water will not drain and air is excluded. The first priority, therefore, is to replace the lost calcium and after the 1953 floods the Government arranged a free supply of gypsum wherever needed at a rate of about 2 tons per acre. Some badly contaminated land needed a further application later in the year and probably an initial spread of 4 tons an acre everywhere would have been ideal with subsequent applications up to 8 to 10 tons per acre where needed. But merely conjuring up the lesser amounts at short notice was difficult, let alone getting it to the required sites. It often had to be dumped at a distance, rain sometimes made it unmanageable and actually spreading the stuff required ingenuity when the structure of the soil was likely to be damaged by undue treading or the use of heavy equipment.

As for the long and tedious business of making homes habitable again and the worrying problem of who was going to pay, money was pouring into the Lord Mayor's Fund from private individuals and public bodies. There was the usual unsettling delay during which the democratic but slow moving processes of central Government considered its policy on the matter, and not till 19 February was a statement issued. The Government agreed to match private generosity to the Lord Mayor's Fund on a £1 for £1 basis and to pay for emergency feeding, clearance of mud and debris, and first aid repair to houses to make them habitable again. Rotting foodstuffs, ruined sticks of furniture whose glue had dissolved in the seawater, and sodden upholstery were bulldozed from the streets or carried away on improvised sledges when the quagmires of unmade roads proved unable to carry heavy vehicles. Water taps and tanks were sterilised, broken gas pipes mended, thousands of electric motors and domestic appliances dried and tested before re-use and gallons of disinfectant were standing freely available in the streets to help clean homes of the unbelievable filth. Canvey Isle had been closed except for authorised workers for the first fortnight after the flood, but when people started to return the reality of conditions in their homes was often far worse than they had imagined. Some had to be treated for hysteria and shock.

The weather turned fine from the middle of February till the middle of March, and sunny days and warm wind, aided by RAF engine heaters, enabled everyone to make great progress. On Canvey Isle houses were generally reparable, though the contents were only fit for disposal, and this was possibly because the bungalows usually had gardens around them which allowed the water a surrounding route. At Harwich, in contrast, far more substantial houses proved to be beyond repair because the foundations on a sandy subsoil had been underscoured by water. Where there had been contamination of flood water by sewage, plaster sometimes had to be ripped from walls and floorboards replaced.

The administrative task of ensuring that it was safe to allow people back

113

into their homes and of certifying their claims for financial aid was enormous and officials drawn from unaffected boroughs were helping on that job for months. It was particularly difficult for them to persuade householders that it was a waste of time using their grant of money on re-decorating their homes too soon. Salt is hygroscopic, which means that it absorbs water vapour from the air. Bricks and wood which have been impregnated by sea water gradually dried out by evaporation but the salt was only drawn very slowly to the surface where it lay like a white powder and could be brushed off. But it took a very long time for house walls to be quite free of salt and while any remained it absorbed water vapour from the air so that persistent dampness ruined decorations. It was hard to accept this and many people were not prepared to believe it. They got their money grants only if they signed away the right to any further grant, and some people later regretted their haste. The more successful decorations were mounted on battening, which reduced the overall measurements of the rooms by a few centimetres but allowed a beneficial air circulation next to the walls.

Gradually over the next months homes became habitable, industry got back to normal and communications were restored. Little could be accomplished that year by market gardeners who lost almost everything that had been flooded, except asparagus which seemed unaffected by the salt. The growers spent the year repairing and re-soiling their glass houses and using Government grants to improve their land with tile drains.

Fruit farmers found their soft fruit bushes either killed outright or so badly damaged that they had to be dug out after a poor summer crop. Cherry trees had often died by the end of March but the effect of sea flooding on apples, pears and plums was often delayed for months or years and farmers were still grubbing out trees three years later.

Arable crops recovered in inverse proportion to the extent of the area flooded. Northumberland managed to raise crops on nearly all its flooded sites during 1953, but Essex with more than 15,000 acres flooded managed to crop only 2 per cent in 1953 and 17 per cent in 1954. East Suffolk and Kent made relatively slow comebacks but the remaining counties were almost back to normal by 1954. Farmers chose their first crops with consideration, barley being popular because of its tolerance to salt. Perennial weeds flourished, unfortunately, because of caution in cultivating the ground too soon in 1953 and many salt-loving weeds not usually found inland appeared in the following years. Grass recovered well wherever flood water subsided quickly but in places like the marshland behind Breydon Water—where water lay for about six weeks because the normal sluices had been purposely sandbagged to prevent flooding back into Yarmouth—the land was left with something like 20 tons of salt per acre and there was little grass in 1953 and only patchy grass in 1954. Moreover there was a lack of mineral content in grass for some time and this had to be made good by special licks for the animals. Peculiar complaints sometimes arose amongst livestock, like the peeling white skin suffered by Friesians which vets could not recognise and has not occurred since. It could have been a grass fever or due to salt weeds or some quite different reaction to sunlight.

All things considered, the storm of 1 February 1953 may well retain the reputation of causing the worst weather disaster of the century, and it is to be hoped that it does, for condi-

114

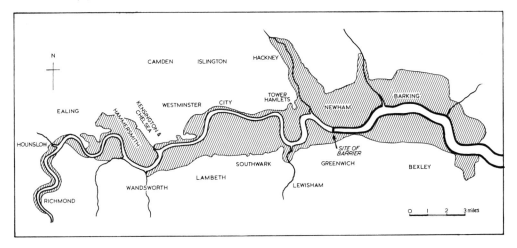

Areas bordering the river Thames in London which are below the 1953 tide level. *(Department of Public Health Engineering)*

tions were still not as bad then as they might have been. High tide was not the highest predicted for the year; only at Harwich did the sea surge nearly coincide with high water. Elsewhere the sea surge came after high tide, except in the Thames Estuary where it preceeded high water by about three hours; and the flow of fresh water down the rivers into the North Sea was not excessive that night. It is the nagging worry that a similar storm might coincide with the highest spring tide of the year and at the same time as river floods are pressing towards the sea from inland which opens such frightening possibilities. Meteorologically speaking, there is no reason why a North Sea surge caused by a depression could not occur at the same time as snow thaw floods like those of 1947.

The immediate reaction to the 1953 floods was to set up a comprehensive Storm Tide Warning Service for the whole of the east coast, operated by the tidal branch of the Admiralty's hydrographic department and the Met Office from the latter's central forecasting office at Bracknell. The coast line is now divided into sections with approximately the same tidal heights, each section having a port of reference at which automatic tide recorders transmit as many times a day as the weather dictates. Assessment of trouble is a complicated affair involving contours of land and off-shore banks, many of which had actually been altered in the storm, as well as the current meteorological situation.

Two kinds of warning are issued: an Alert 12 hours before high water at the port of reference, and a Danger signal issued 4 hours before high water if the previous *possibility* warning becomes a *probability*. Warnings are sent direct to river boards who in turn advise the police about possible consequences. The police pass on the information as deemed necessary so that ships' moorings can be tended, sandbags lined up in readiness and lookouts posted on the sea defences. Warnings are not issued direct to the public—it only needs one instance of moving cattle to higher ground in the middle of the night because of a flood warning which fails to materialise and the risk is shrugged off when the next warning is received. In the midst of the outcry, after the 1953 floods, that no warnings had been given in time, there were many people who admitted they had been warned but had taken no heed.

There have been alerts since that 1953 storm and there will be more. One occurred in the middle of January 1974 when all the heavenly bodies were conspiring together to produce particularly high tides. The east coast prayed not to have a depression with northerly gales in the North Sea, so it was curious to read the newspaper headlines of 14 January, 'Gales save London from threat of disaster'. Gales *had* materialised but from a westerly direction, thus helping to hold back tides which might have swamped the Thames estuary.

The engineered walls along the east coast were rebuilt where necessary and it became a cardinal principle of reconstruction that the insides should be given as much attention as the outsides. Grass was extensively used to bind the soil on the inside but particularly susceptible stretches were faced on both sides with engineered, often hexagonal, blocks. Where the defence lines could be shortened by damming creeks along the Essex coast without upsetting too many other interests, this was done.

And the race against time to finish the Thames Barrier proceeds in earnest. By the middle of 1975 the piers which will support the pivoting flood gates built side by side across the river at Woolwich were driven into the Thames. The cost of building it has escalated from £75 million when the plan received Royal Assent in 1972 to £170 million by the end of 1974 and continuing inflation raises apprehension about what the further rise in cost may be. But if London is to continue to live with reasonable peace of mind the work must go on. Look at the map on p115 showing the area of the capital below Trinity High Water and below the level of the tide on 1 February 1953 and imagine what would happen if the defences broke down during a surge flood alone or in combination with a thaw flood. The work is scheduled for completion by 1978 and London will be on tenterhooks till it is accomplished.

10

The heaven is shut up and there is no rain

2 Chronicles 6.26

So far the 'baddies' of this book have all been depressions, because most weather disasters are caused by gales or excessive rain and these are the prerogative of low pressure systems. The high pressure circulations, called anticyclones, are in comparison sluggish and non-violent but this does not make them invariably 'goodies'. They too have their nasty ways of inflicting disaster.

Surface friction has the same effect in an anticyclone as in a depression and causes wind near the ground to be backed in direction from that at 600m above ground. But since wind blows in a clockwise direction round centres of high pressure, the backing tendency causes an outflow of air near the ground. This divergence leads to subsidence of air over the centre of the anticyclone, which causes air to warm because of compression and thereby increase its capacity for water vapour. Air nibbles moisture from the upper clouds which evaporate and eventually disappear altogether, leaving free access for the sun to warm the ground all day but also permitting heat to radiate outwards into space during the night. Anticyclones, therefore, give heat waves during the summer and very cold spells during the winter. Temperatures in Britain, however, never reach the extremes experienced over large continents because of the abundant moisture due to its island position in the depression tracks. There is usually some depression ready and able to take over from an anticyclone after a few weeks, and enough moisture to permit upper air thunderstorms to interrupt a heat wave in summer or fog to blanket against further falls in temperature during the winter.

Whatever the season, the chief characteristic of anticyclones is absence of rain, and though Britain is never likely to come to the brink of starvation because of drought, the increasing demands of industry and a growing population is starting to make careful budgeting of the country's water imperative. There is no way of increasing the average total rainfall, and the wet years must carry the dry years if serious trouble is not to occur. As it is, most years see financial disaster come to some farmers, either because drought comes too early when seeds are supposed to be germinating, or too late when unripened crops have already been ruined by rain. Artificial watering systems are not the whole answer because low reservoirs may lead to the banning of sprinklers at just the time they are needed most.

Lack of rain, however, is only half the problem of a drought because air itself has a thirst for water. When it is not saturated with vapour and therefore spilling out water, it is busy slaking its own thirst from whatever source it can find. These are obviously rivers, streams, ponds or wet washing on the lines and also the less obvious sources, such as twigs, grass, leaves, window frames and roof timbers, which yield up their minute quantities of water and become tinder dry and vulnerable to fire. This dryness is dangerous at all seasons but obviously more so in summer when high air temperatures increase the rate of evaporation. Carelessly thrown matches or sunlight focussed through broken glass set alight acres of countryside every heat wave. Fortunately nature is resilient and charred land usually recovers and is often improved, but buildings have no reproductive powers. The years of drought before meteorological records were kept can be deduced from references in parish records to collections for fire victims, repair and purchase of firebuckets and firehooks for pulling down burning roofs. Generally speaking, wind near the centres of anticyclones is light or calm and fires need not spread far if attended quickly. But on the outer fringes of anticyclones, where they start to blend in with the low pressure systems but still retain their high pressure weather, wind can blow as fiercely as near the centre of depressions. This turned a simple fire in London into the worst fire disaster the country has ever known.

Fire of London   September 1666
By the middle of the seventeenth century London was a city of closely packed houses whose upper floors reached over the streets, almost touching the ones opposite in an endeavour to gain extra living space. The

streets were gloomy tunnels into which sunshine hardly penetrated, buildings were mainly of wood, and fires were frequent enough to cause many people forebodings of disaster. Several petitions to King Charles I for practical and financial insurance against fire had been made but nothing resulted. Firehooks and buckets were kept ready in churches, people were urged to have buckets of water in their homes and alarm was literally dampened by four wet summers between 1660 and 1664, when there were fewer fires than usual. The year of the plague, 1665 was dry and the number of fires again increased. The summer of 1666 was dominated by anticyclones and by late summer many rivers and streams were dry.

On 2 September 1666, a fresh east wind was blowing and every building in London was bone dry. About 2am a small fire started in Pudding Lane near London Bridge, and the baker's

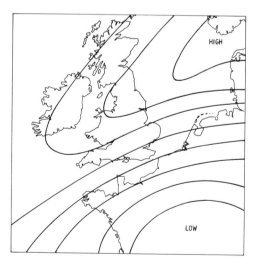

Probable weather chart at the time of the Great Fire of London in September 1666. The high pressure ridge was dominant as far as weather was concerned, it being fine and dry, but a depression over western Europe was probably deepening to give a steeper pressure gradient and strong wind over London.

118

man was not awakened till the house was full of smoke. The fire spread gradually down the street till it reached Thames Street where it was fed by hay, timber and coals on open wharves and by inflammable stocks of tallow, oil, spirits and hemp in the warehouses. The whistling east wind drove the now immense fire ahead of it and no authoritative person was inclined to interrupt his day of rest to deal with what was probably just another outbreak. By the end of Sunday flames engulfed almost the whole area between Cannon Street and Queenhithe Dock on the river, and the narrow streets were jammed with inhabitants seeking refuge and pushing carts loaded with their possessions.

By Monday morning, still fine and windy, it was obvious that this was no ordinary fire and the Duke of York took control. Soldiers, seamen and constables were recruited into fire-fighting teams and they worked valiantly to pull down burning houses and blow up others in order to create a fire barrier. The wind simply laughed at them and snatched up burning embers and carried them across the fire barriers to the supposedly protected buildings beyond. Water became non-existent. The streams and wells were low anyhow and everywhere people had torn up roads and cut into the hollow elm trunks which served as water pipes in order to fill their buckets. Most water ran to waste. A pall of smoke trailed for miles downwind under a typical anticyclonic temperature inversion and as the sun struggled to penetrate the smoke the afternoon glowed weirdly red. By the end of Monday the wind had pushed the fire beyond Cornhill in the north and to the end of Thames Street near Blackfriars. The streets at night were illuminated by flames as if by sunshine.

On Tuesday the wind backed a little to ENE but was even stronger. By evening St Paul's had been devoured, fire had driven along Newgate and Ludgate Hill and hopes of limiting it faded in despair. But the wind too had exhausted its energy and late on Tuesday night it fell calm before veering south on Wednesday. The flames were got under control but it was not the end of the fires. Many cellars and closed buildings had been heated enormously during the four days without actually igniting and, despite a rainy spell which started on 9 September and almost incessant heavy rain for ten days in early October, these danger spots often came to life during the next few months.

The Great Fire of London destroyed 13,000 houses, churches and public buildings, valued at about £7-10 million and not insured. There was extraordinarily little loss of life, partly because buildings were low enough for people to jump to safety, but mainly because the fire was driven along a predictable path so that people could see when their turn was about to come. Four deaths were known to have occurred, possibly eight, but several of these could have been murders by a panic stricken populace furious at rumours that the fire had been started by their enemies, the French, the Dutch or, more generally, the Catholics.

London was rebuilt — over a much longer period than the boastful three years inscribed on the commemorative Monument in the City — with wider streets and using brick and stone. The final result did not conform to all the hopeful planning standards set but it was certainly an improvement and considerably more hygienic. Fire insurance did not get started until 1680 and, though a renewed interest was taken in the kind of fire engines that

James Colquon of Edinburgh built in 1650 for that city and for Glasgow, precautionary measures developed very slowly. Nothing prevented another disastrous fire at Wapping on 19 November 1682 when the homes of 1500 families were destroyed. Newsham of London built the first successful fire engine in England in 1721 which was adopted by most big cities, and the steam fire engine was developed about 1858. A proper fire service such as Britain has today is only about 150 years old.

A modern fire brigade would undoubtedly have contained the Pudding Lane fire even with the aggravation of a driving dry horizontal wind, but there is no reason for complacency about the risk of disastrous fires. The same shortage of living space which caused London to huddle too closely together in 1666 has in the twentieth century led to taller and taller buildings on the restricted ground space. Once started, a fire spreads quickly upwards, and occupants must flee from one floor to the next higher till there is only the roof to get on to. This may be out of reach of ladders, too high to jump from, and will probably burn too hotly for a helicopter rescue. Ghastly tragedies have happened this way abroad and only the most stringent fire precautions will prevent it happening sometime in Britain.

Moreover, one large fire, or perhaps several spread by the wind, can create its own disastrous 'weather', independent of either depression or anticyclone which the weather map reveals. The convection currents soaring above such a fire can be violent enough to suck in replacement air towards the centre and cause winds far greater than normal. The classic example occurred during the destruction of Dresden in the war when fire storm winds developed into tornadoes, and uprooted trees and hurled people fleeing *from* the fire backwards into the very centre of it. Huge fires at some of Britain's industrial centres could do just the same thing and, once started, firefighting apparatus would be helpless.

London smog   December 1952

It may seem odd that the anticyclones which lead to excessive dryness in summer can also produce excessive dampness in winter. The vital difference lies with the altitude of the sun which gives only feeble warmth during a short day followed by a long night during which heat can radiate away from the earth. The imbalance leads to a progressive fall in temperature at ground level as the anticyclone persists. Eventually air becomes too cold to contain its whole burden of water vapour and some condenses out as fog. If the air is already moist, condensation occurs quite soon after temperature starts to fall. British winters have always had more than their fair share of fog.

During past centuries, when people died younger anyhow, when they had little need to travel at night and the country was basically an agricultural community, the malignant effects of fog were indistinguishable from other hazards of life. As the population settled into large towns and coal fires increased the amount of smoke in the atmosphere, and as the industrial revolution gradually added its belching pollution, the character of fogs changed. They became stinking 'pea soupers', coloured by particles of coal, oil and petrol which were irritating to the lungs and some even poisonous, and they became more frequent because the many nuclei in the air aided the condensation of water vapour. In particular, sulphur dioxide combined with moisture and oxygen to form sulphuric acid in the fog, creating a potent health hazard.

November in 1952 was bitterly cold with considerable snow, and temperatures were already low when an anticyclone established itself over the country in the first week of December. Everyone's coal fires were pouring smoke up their chimneys in the great effort to keep homes warm. Fog formed on 5 December, there was no hope of the miserable sun clearing it the next day and the anticyclone had no intention of moving away to permit a clearing airstream. The easterly wind drift was the worst direction for adding industrial pollutants to the air over London and the fog got yellower and yellower. It pressed upon the windows like a malignant enemy, it seeped through doors to make it even difficult to see clearly inside and it brought traffic almost to a standstill. A new word was born into the vocabulary—'smog' and the smog persisted till 9 December. It is remembered by those who survived as a period of maddening claustrophobia, but probably 4000 people died because of it. I say 'probably' because the certified causes of death were usually bronchitis or pneumonia, but the fact that the number of deaths for these reasons were more than seven times the normal pointed to fog being the primary culprit.

Those who had been campaigning against smoke pollution had their case most disturbingly reinforced. A Committee on Air Pollution resulted in the Clean Air Act of 1956, since when industry and homes have been required to convert by stages to smokeless fuels and control the emission of black smoke. It has not, and cannot, prevent fog forming altogether but the policy seems to be paying off. Fog has been less frequent and less persistent during the 1960s and the 1970s and they have been reverting in type to the white country fogs. Perhaps the word smog will eventually only be used to describe that one particularly disastrous occasion of 1952.

Motorway pile-up 30 November 1971
Transport is a necessary part of commercial life, business appointments will not wait and few people can afford to stay off the roads altogether just because of fog. Every time there is thick fog there are accidents because people drive too fast. It is not enough to put this down to 'motorway madness'. No one really embarks upon a journey with suicidal intent but with a positive desire to reach a destination. The trouble is much more likely to be deprivation of normal visual aids for judging speed. Lampposts and houses can no longer be seen passing across the peripheral vision of the eye, and drivers are concentrating so hard on what lies ahead, perhaps

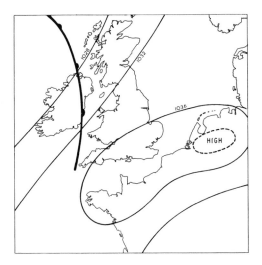

0600 GMT 7 December 1952, the third day of fog which persisted till 9 December. Industrial pollution turned the fog into 'smog' and caused many deaths amongst the old and ailing.

121

the tail light of another car, that they dare not take their eyes off the screen to watch the speedometer.

By far the most dangerous time is when fog is starting to form or when it is dispersing, because visibility can change so abruptly from extremely good to nothing at all. Tarmac, concrete and green fields all respond at different rates to heat from the sun or radiation cooling at night and therefore there are always corresponding differences in air temperature along any stretch of road. Moreover, quantities of water vapour in the air also vary — towns are always drier, for instance, than open fields — and quite gentle contours of ground hold tempting hollows into which cold air drains eagerly.

It had been foggy in the early morning of 30 November 1971 and the fog lights had been showing on the M1. But by 11am the sun had broken through, the warning lights had been switched off and the day was bright enough, despite the season, for drivers on the motorway near Luton to be wearing their sunglasses. The usual mixture of busy traffic was streaming in either direction: bulk liquid tankers, heavy articulated lorries, private cars with chatting families and lone drivers relieving the monotony of the journey with music from their radios. They were all driving at speeds for which the motorway was built and everything seemed well with the world and perfectly normal.

Then a laggard patch of fog from the adjacent fields responded to the winter sunshine, stirred upwards from the grass and drifted in the light breeze across the motorway. Someone reacted instinctively to the sudden blindness by braking, the vehicle behind ran into his rear, the next lorry did the same . . . and the next . . . and the next. Some drivers were able to jump clear

On 29 November 1971 night fog cleared during the morning to give normal motoring conditions in bright sunshine on the M1. Then a strip of fog belatedly stirred itself from the adjacent fields and drifted across the motorway. Someone braked and the following vehicles piled into one another. When sunshine returned the scene resembled a breaker's yard. *(Daily Mirror)*

and run down the embankment away from the continuing crashes they could hear behind them; other people were trapped fast in their crumpled shells of metal and several others were killed outright and never saw the grim scene revealed when sunlight returned a short while later. The motorway looked like a breaker's yard: about fifty vehicles were piled up on the southbound carriageway and twenty or so on the northbound lanes. There were cries and screams from all quarters.

Those who were free and uninjured tried to help the less fortunate. An ambulance driver who had been taking patients to Luton hospital for routine treatment stopped to do what he could in the more urgent situation he found himself in, but there was very little that could be accomplished until rescue workers arrived with metal cutting equipment and cranes. That in itself was a major operation because of the trail of wreckage blocking the road in both directions and the queue of traffic building up without knowing the cause. Some of the trapped people had to wait up to five hours before being released and the sad toll of the few moments' holocaust was seven people dead and forty-five injured.

Comments after the accident reflected the complexity of these motorway pile-ups which had occured before and have happened since. Someone was said to have 'panicked' by braking when he encountered the fog patch — if it had been merely a will o' the wisp scarf across the road through which he could have seen sunshine beyond, then this might have been considered a fair description. But the patch was substantial, enough to be totally blinding, and it seems a moot point whether in those circumstances it is more panicky to brake than to continue at the same speed.

A police officer thought that if people had been driving properly they would have seen the blanket of fog ahead in time to slow down, but this seems to underestimate the masking effect of three lanes of traffic ahead on which one is concentrating.

There were ideas galore for better warning systems; many of such sophistication that they would be financially crippling to install, and mostly ignoring the basic problem of any fog warning system: how to get people to appreciate what the warning is about. It may indicate that there *is* fog ahead, and then motorists ignore the statement of fact at their peril and should be prosecuted accordingly. But the warning must sometimes also mean that there are *some* patches of fog ahead, or even that conditions are ripe for fog to form but they have not done so yet; in which case it is impossible to locate the danger or even guarantee that it exists. Hence warning lights may be associated with false information when no fog actually materialises, and they are treated with contempt on the next occasion when the worst may happen. Even supposing the potential risk is fully appreciated, is it feasible to expect motorists to cruise along at a cautious low speed when visibility is perfect?

Probably the final answer will be some sort of radar 'eye' to enable a motorist to 'see' in fog as well as in clear air. Of one thing I am certain, there can never be a professional forecast accurate enough in detail to pinpoint the place and timing of a fog bank precisely. A forecast can assess the liability to fog in general terms but anticipating the final tip of balance from good visibility to opaque fog must always remain the responsibility of the person on the spot.

In varying degrees, the final assessment of danger from *any* weather situation lies with the individual. If we are ever to beat the weather at its own game we must educate ourselves to learn its habits and read accurately the language of the barometer, the clouds or the deceptive benignity of early morning sunshine and brilliant starry nights.

BIBLIOGRAPHY

Abbreviations:
W   *Weather* (magazine)
MM   *Meteorological Magazine*
BRS   *Building Research Station* (digest)
GJ   *Geographical Journal*
GM   *Geophysical Memoir*

WIND

Menzies, J. B.   Wind damage to buildings in the UK 1962-1969   *BRS*

Wilson, P. H.   Glasgow wind damage *BRS*

Newberry & Wise   How wind shapes buildings   *BRS*

Newberry, C. W.   Significant features of wind loading   *BRS*

BRS 99, 101   Wind loading on buildings

BRS 119   Assessment of wind loads

Newberry, C. W.   Wind uplift on a low pitched roof   *BRS*

Aanensen, C. J. M.   Gales in Yorkshire *GM* 108 Met O

Aanensen & Sawyers   Gale of Feb 16th, 1962, in Yorkshire   *Nature* 197

Booth, B. J.   The *Royal Charter*   *W* Dec 1970

Fitzroy, R.   *Weather Book*

Shellard, H. C.   Collapse of cooling towers, Ferrybridge   *W* June 1967

Carr Laughton & Heddon   *Great Storms*

Defoe, D.   *The Great Storm 1703*

TORNADOES

Lamb, H. H.   Tornadoes in England *GM* 99 Met O

Gilbert & Walker   Tornado at Royal Horticultural Garden Wisley   *W* June 1966

Radford, J. A.   Tornado at RHS Gardens Wisley   *W* June 1966

Guide to Parish Church at Widecombe-in-the-Moor

Tagg, J. R.   Tornado at Cranfield, 26 June 1973   *W* Feb 1974

Meaden, G. T.   Four storm stories from Steeple Ashton   *W* Dec 1973

Bonacina, L. C. W.   Widecombe Calamity   *W* 1946

Botley, C.   Widecombe Calamity   *W* Sept 1966

Wright, P. B.   Tornado in south Yorkshire, and others   *W* Oct 1973

Lane, F.   *The Elements Rage*

FRESH-WATER FLOODS

Wood, H.   Norwich flood 1912 *London Jnl Royal Sanitary Inst*   42, 1922

City of Norwich   *Illustrated Record of the Great Flood Aug 1912*

Learmouth, A. T. A.   *Floods of 12th Aug 1948 in south east Scotland*

Glasspole & Douglas   Tweed Valley floods *MM* Jan 1949

Newnham, E. V.   Disastrous floods at Louth May 29, 1920   *Met O Notes 17*

Hanwell & Newson   *Great Storms and Floods July 1928 on Mendips*

Bleasdale & Douglas   Storm over Exmoor Aug 15 1952   *MM* Dec 1952

Bonacina, L. C. W.   The Exmoor cataclysm   *W* Nov 1952

Kidson, C.   The Exmoor storm and Lynmouth floods   *Geographia* 1953

Delderfield, E. R.   *The Lynmouth Flood Disaster*

David & Charles (publishers) *Devon Flood Story 1960*

Cross, D. A. E.   Great Till Flood Jan 1841   *W* June 1966

HMSO   *Harvest Home*

Welland River Board   *R Welland Major Improvement Scheme 1947-57*

Salter, P. R. S.   Heavy rain of 10 July 1968   *MM* March 1969

SALT-WATER FLOODS

Argles & Montgomery   Nursing flooded orchards back to health   *Grower* Feb 1953

Pizer, N. H.   Reclamation of land from sea   *Chemistry & Industry* May 1966

Jenkins, W. L.   Tidal Rivers & Floods   *Jnl Inst of Sanitary Engineers 32*, 1938

GLC report   *Taming the Thames*

Lennox Kerr, J.   *The Great Storm*

Grieve, H.   *The Great Tide* (definitive history of 1953 storm) Essex Record 1959

Douglas, C. K. M.   Gale of Jan 31st, 1953   *MM* April 1953

Reynolds, G.   Storm Surge research   *W* April 1953

Jenson, H. A. P.   Tidal inundations past and present   *W* April 1953

Bowden, K. F.   Storm surges in North Sea   *W* April 1953

Quales & Ufford   Disastrous storm surge of Feb 1   *W* April 1953

Steers, J. A.   East coast floods 1953   *GJ* 1953

Valentin, H.   Present vertical movements of the B Isles   *GJ* 1953

Mirrlees, S. T. A.   Thames floods of Jan 7, 1928   *MM* Feb 1928

Carruthers, J. N.   Horsey floods of Feb 1938   *MM* May 1938

Lennon, G.W.   Weather conditions and storm surges on west coast British Isles   *Quarterly Jrnl R Met Soc*

SNOW, FROST, COLD

Plasschaert, J. H. M.   Weather and avalanches   *W* Mar 1969

Canovan, R. A.   Wintry prospects for British Rail   *W* Nov 1971

Manley, G.   Snowfall in Britain over past 300 years   *W* Nov 1969

Clarke, P. C.   Snowfalls over south east England 1954-69   *W* Nov 1969

Lyall, I. T.   Low temperatures in southern Britain   1953-72   *W* Apr 1973

Lyall, I. T.   English winters since 1950   *W* Oct 1971

Rigg, J. B.   Influence of local conditions on freezing of Thames   *W* Feb 1964

Millington, R. A.   Physiological responses to cold   *W* Nov 1964

Hurst & Lenz   Earth temperature changes winter 1962-63   *W* Apr 1964

Booth, R. E.   Looking back on 1963   *W* Sept 1964

Green, F. H. W.   Weather in north Scotland Jan/Feb 1963   *W* Dec 1963

Brooks & Douglas   Glazed frost of January 1940   *GM* 98 Met O

Shellard, H. C.   Winter 1962-63 in U.K.   *MM* May 1968

Douglas, C. K. M.   Severe winter 1946-47   *MM* Mar 1947

Andrews, W.   *Famous Frosts and Frost Fairs*

Carter, C.   *The Blizzard of '91*   David & Charles 1971

Fraser, C.   *The Avalanche Enigma*   Murray 1966

Sussex Express pamphlet *Lewes Avalanche 1836*

Small, T. V.   Icing at sea   *JRNSS* 6 vol 26

De-icing equipment tested in arctic waters *Fishing News International* Mar 1969

CLIMATE

Chandler, T. J.   *The Climate of London*

Brazell, J. H.   *London Weather*   HMSO

Lamb, H. H.   *The English Climate*

MISCELLANEOUS

Bell, W. G.   *Great Fire of London 1666*

The Times, Daily Telegraph, Glasgow Herald

125

INDEX

Abbey St Bathans, 55
Anticyclone, 117
Avalanche, 85

Barometer, 30, 35
Berkshire, 25-7
Blizzard, 71, 75-7, 80
Boston Phantom, 79
Boston Typhoon, 78
Breeches buoy, 76, 101
Bridges, 10-11, 35, 44-6, 52-6, 63-8
Bristol, 33
Buildings, 8-10, 12-15, 17-23, 34, 45, 56,
    63-8, 104-8

Canvey Isle, 105-6, 110
Cairngorms, 70-3
Capsize, 18, 77, 101-3
Charts, 6, 16, 30, 35, 38
Cheddar Gorge, 60
Chimneys, 12, 17-19, 34-5
Clean Air Act, 121
Cloud, lenticular, 14; funnel, 24-5, 28, 57;
    rain, 38; shower, 24
Cloud burst, 57
Coastguard, 102
Cobham, 46
Cold front, 38
Convection, 38
Convergence, 38
Cooling towers, 8-10
Cornice, 70, 86
Cornwall, 75-7
Cumledge, 54

Dam, 56, 58, 67
Debris, 52-6, 61, 63-7
Defoe, D., 33-7
Depression, 16, 21-3, 29, 69, 74
Derham, W., 35
Devon, 57-60, 67-8, 75-7
Divergence, 117
Dog, 70
Downs, 33-4
Drains, 41-3, 48, 61
Drought, 117

Drying machines, 90-4, 103-4
Dundee, 10
Dykes, 90-4, 103-4

Earthquake, 5, 20
East Anglia, 90-95
East coast, 103-16
Eddystone, 30, 33
Eliot, Admiral, 30
Enzymes, 72
Essex, 103-16
Exeter, 68
Exmoor, 61-8
Exposure, 72
Eye (hurricane), 21; (river), 52

Fens, 90-5
Ferrybridge, 8-10
Fire, 118-20
Firestorm, 120
Fitzroy, Admiral, 30-2; remarks, 31
Floods, rain, 39-68; thaw, 20, 88-95; sea,
    103-16
Fog, 120-23
Forecast, 5-6, 15, 23, 50, 70, 73, 79, 81
Frost Fair, 83
Fungus, 50

Gales, on land, 6-11, 12-23, 35-7, 92; at sea,
    11, 29-37, 75
Glasgow, 16-23
Glazed frost, 86-8
Goodwins, 33-4

Hansy, 29-30
Hatfield, 6-8
Helicopter, 12, 72, 81
Holland, 108
Hull, 77-9
Hurricane, 5, 21-2, 30-2
Hypothermia, 84

Ice, 73, 77-80, 86-8; black, 81-2; collars, 87;
    floes 82, 86, 93
Insulation, 76
Isobars, 5-6, 13-14, 16, 77

Jaywick, 104-5

Lammermuir Hills, 52-4
Lewes, 85
Lea, river, 90-3
Lifeboat, 75, 102
Lightning, 24-7
Linslade, 26
London, 35, 82, 93, 97-100, 116, 118-21
Low Countries, 50, 75
Luton, 121-3
Lynmouth, 61-7
Lynton, 61-7

Maplethorpe, 107
Medway, river, 90
Mendips, 60
Mole, river, 45-51
Molesey, 46-51
Mossdale, 39-40
Motorway madness, 121

Norwich, 43-5
Norwood, 40
Notts County, 79

Oil rig, 11, 20
Otter, river, 58-9

Pennines, 12-15
Plynlimon, 87
Ponding, *see* dam
Pothole, 39
Pressure, atmospheric, 5-6, 16, 27, 30, 31,
    38; explosive, 25-6
Pumps, 41-2, 67, 90, 94

Rain, 38-9
River banks, 51, 54, 97-100; *see also* dykes
Roofs, 5-8, 12, 19-20, 26, 35
Ross Cleveland, 77-9
Royal Charter, 30-2

Salt, 112-14
Scilly Isles, 76
Scotland, 52-3, 100-3
Sea Gem, 11-12
Sea Quest, 20
Sea walls, 103-12, 116
Severn river, 33
Sheffield, 12-15
Shipwrecks, 29; *Bay of Panama,* 76; *Clan
    Macquarrie,* 101; *Hansy,* 29; naval, 34;
    Princess Victoria, 101-3; *Royal Charter,*
    30-32
Shipping bulletins, 23, 31-2
Shovell, Admiral, 33
Smog, 120

Snow, 69-72, 75-7, 85, 89-90; caves, 71-7;
    plough, 75, 81; thaw, 85
Snowdon Mt, 70, 73-4
Snowdrop Inn, 86
Soil, drainage, 39-40, 50; erosion, 55;
    structure, 112
Somerset, 57-61, 67-8
Stuttgart, 80
Stranraer, 100-2
Subsidence, 117
Surbiton, 41-3
Surge, 96, 104-16
Sutton on Sea, 108

Taunton, 68
Tay Bridge, 10-11
Temperature, air, 14, 74, 82; body, 72;
    river, 83; sea, 69
Thames barrier, 100-16
Thames river, 33-4, 49, 86, 90, 97-100
Thaw, 85, 88, 90
Tides, 96-100, 115-16
Till river, 88
Tornado, 22-9, 35, 57
Trees, 24, 37, 66, 75, 101
Trough, 38-9

Vermuyden, C, 90

Walton, 47
Warm front, 38
Water spout, 57
Whitadder, 54
Whiteout, 71
Widecombe-in-the-Moor, 27-8
Wind, 6, 9, 16, 38; changes, 31; funnelling,
    23; gusts, 9-11; suction, 7, 35; surface, 6,
    38; turbulence, 13; undulation, 13
Wind tunnel, 8, 10
Winter, 80-4
Wisley, 24

127